OVERCOMING
PHOBIAS

PATRICIA FURNESS-SMITH

A PRACTICAL GUIDE

Published in the UK and USA
in 2014 by Icon Books Ltd,
Omnibus Business Centre,
39–41 North Road,
London N7 9DP
email: info@iconbooks.net
www.iconbooks.net

Sold in the UK, Europe and Asia
by Faber & Faber Ltd,
Bloomsbury House,
74–77 Great Russell Street,
London WC1B 3DA
or their agents

Distributed in South Africa
by Book Promotions,
Office B4, The District,
41 Sir Lowry Road,
Woodstock 7925

Distributed in Australia and
New Zealand
by Allen & Unwin Pty Ltd,
PO Box 8500,
83 Alexander Street,
Crows Nest,
NSW 2065

Distributed in Canada
by Penguin Books Canada,
90 Eglinton Avenue East, Suite 700,
Toronto,
Ontario M4P 2Y3

Distributed to the trade in the USA
by Consortium Book Sales
and Distribution
The Keg House,
34 Thirteenth Avenue NE, Suite 101,
Minneapolis, MN 55413-1007

ISBN: 978-184831-650-8

About the Author

Patricia Furness-Smith is an international phobia specialist with a particular interest in Hodophobia, the fear of travelling. For over ten years she has worked as a consultant on British Airways' 'Flying with Confidence' courses where she has helped thousands of sufferers overcome their fear of flying and has recently had published a book on this subject. She is often quoted in the media and has appeared in national newspapers and magazines and on social media sites, radio and television.

Her career includes over twenty years' experience in lecturing and training in psychology, psychopathology and psychotherapy in further and higher education across a variety of institutions, including prisons and financial establishments. She is a fellow of the Institute for Learning and a Fellow of the Chartered Institute of Educational Assessors. She is also a member of a validation panel for a leading supervision training provider.

Her other specialisms are working with eating disorders and relationship therapy, having been involved in these fields for almost 25 years with leading national and local providers.

She is a Fellow of the National Counselling Society and runs her own practice in Buckinghamshire where she offers individual therapy for all mental health issues, couple therapy and workplace therapeutic services.

Author's Note

I have changed the names of all the people I have described in case studies. In order to respect privacy and anonymity, I have scrambled some of the personal details and have formed composite characters.

Dedication

I would like to dedicate this book to my extraordinary mother-in-law, Joan Barbara Gilbert (née Rapsey), a veritable legend in her own lifetime, and my dear father-in-law, John Gerald Furness-Smith. I thank them for all the wonderful times we have shared over the past 40 years, their unstinting support, amazing generosity and singular brand of humour. But most of all I am eternally grateful to them for producing their son, Charles, the love of my life.

Contents

Preface

Difficulties are things that show a person what they are.
Epictetus

From as far back as I can remember I have always been intrigued by the human mind. That curiosity has led me into a career where I have been privileged to gain access to the personal experiences of thousands of people. My clients and students, over the past 25 years, have generously and courageously shared with me the deepest and darkest recesses of their minds.

Throughout these many years of exploration I have come to realize that each of us possesses huge reservoirs of untapped resources. One of the joys I experience in my work is that I am able to alert my clients and students to the fact that they all have amazing potential if only they choose to recognize this fact.

In this book I hope to convince you that overcoming life-long limiting phobias is readily achievable, providing you have an open mind, a willingness to learn and the courage to try new ways of thinking and behaving.

Very little of what we think about ourselves is actually based on indisputable solid concrete evidence; so why not elect to have positive and constructive thoughts rather than limiting and debilitating ones. After all, beyond the certainty that everyone reading this book has been born and one day will die – all else is mere speculation.

As we embark upon this adventure into the world of phobias I want you to keep these pre-requisites to change in the forefront of your mind.

In many ways a book entitled *Overcoming Phobias* might imply that the objective is to return the reader to the status quo, which existed before they became afflicted with the phobia. From my experience, in this field, I can categorically say that this is only half the story. History records endless examples of individuals who have overcome serious personal challenges and afflictions to emerge as stronger, more resilient and resourceful versions of their former selves. Winston Churchill, Helen Keller and Bob Champion are just a few who, through conquering adversity, went on to accomplish incredible achievements.

The wonderful by-product of overcoming a phobia is that it not only releases you from your 'imprisonment' but it will imbue you with tremendous inner confidence which will enable you to soar to even higher levels of personal achievement and satisfaction.

In the following chapters I will provide you with the knowledge and information you need to work towards defeating a phobia; but only you can provide the attitudes of determination and openness to put this learning into action. I hope that you accept this invitation to work together to enable you to discover how truly amazing you are.

Introduction

Fear is a tyrant and a despot, more terrible than the rack, more potent than a snake.
Edgar Wallace

A phobia is an intense fear of 'something', such as an object or situation, which would not normally worry others. The person with the phobia knows that they are being irrational and that their response is entirely out of proportion to the threat, but feels powerless and unable to control their negative thoughts and bodily sensations.

A phobia is a type of anxiety disorder, which causes people to adjust their lives in order to avoid encountering the feared 'something'. Phobias range from mild to strong but all are annoying, limiting and frustrating, and some are downright exhausting, debilitating and overwhelmingly terrifying.

Welcome reader to the land of **phobias**. This terrain is populated with the most diverse range of characters in the mental health field. Phobias are very common in the western world and affect many millions of people. The Royal College of Psychiatrists tells us that as many as one in ten people will suffer from a phobia at some point in their lives.

The actual figure is believed to be significantly higher than this with some sources suggesting that as many as 16 million people suffer from phobias in the UK alone.

The reason why we have such a huge discrepancy in these figures is because mental health issues in general are victims of under-reporting, due to the perceived stigma which they attract.

Added to this, phobias by their very nature are irrational fears, therefore frequently cause the sufferer acute shame and embarrassment as well as anxiety and distress. For this reason many people with a phobia do not seek medical help.

Worryingly, evidence shows that the vast majority of people who do eventually seek help for their phobia have endured symptoms for over ten years. Sadly, some sufferers do not even disclose their problems to close family or friends out of fear of being ridiculed or teased, thus rendering them isolated from all avenues of support. The examples below illustrate this point.

Coulrophobia *(Fear of Clowns)*

Imagine how you would feel if your wife informed you that your young daughter had chosen a visit to the circus, with several of her friends, for her seventh birthday treat. How easy would it be to come clean and tell your family that you can't accompany them because you have a terror of clowns?

The chances are that you would probably come up with some elaborate excuse to save you from the embarrassment. But as the saying goes 'liars have to have good memories' so this 'white lie' not only has an energy cost but will also make you feel uncomfortable for not being straight with your loved ones.

Being incongruent, that is, projecting an image which does not tally with how we really feel, becomes an ongoing stressor in our life and inevitably leads to greater anxiety.

Eremikophobia (Fear of Sand)

Your fiancé meets you in the restaurant and presents you with some airline tickets and hotel reservations. He excitedly informs you that he has booked a luxury two-week holiday in the Maldives for your honeymoon in six weeks' time.

In the flush of romance you 'omitted' to mention that you have a phobia of sand! Now what are you going to do? You will have to confront the problem since I am sure that you of all people will not resort to 'burying your head in the sand'!

A phobia is a type of fear and it can literally be a fear of anything. The key aspect of this type of fear is that the threat is actually non-existent or greatly exaggerated.

Phobias are not always taken seriously by others

Many of us are familiar with people having a fear of spiders, heights or enclosed spaces. But how many people have you met who have a fear of uneven seams or a fear of swallowing? In my work I have met these people, whose lives have not only been blighted by such fears but have also encountered contempt, dismissal or disbelief when they have confided in others about their difficulties.

Those of us with physical illnesses are offered understanding and sympathy, but sadly there is still a long distance to be travelled before mental health problems are afforded the same level of comprehension and compassion. In this book I hope to address this imbalance.

 Having a phobia is not your fault and it doesn't mean you are weak; however, being prepared to challenge your phobia and reclaim your autonomy does mean that you are courageous.

People do not go out and freely acquire a phobia any more than we would expect them to willingly become afflicted with heart problems, skin complaints and other physical illnesses. In this book you won't find any trite dismissive phrases like 'it's just a case of mind over matter', 'you'll be okay', 'pull yourself together', and so forth as a response to how to deal with your phobia.

Who will benefit from reading this book?
You may have picked this book up out of pure curiosity or because you are a general practitioner or therapist and wish to know what treatments are available, in order to help your patients or clients. There is a strong possibility that you

yourself may have a phobia or know someone close who is suffering from one. Whoever you are, I am both delighted and excited at the prospect of accompanying you on your journey through this little book.

It is my hope that, by sharing my enthusiasm and experience, you will be empowered to help liberate yourself or others from the stranglehold of phobias. If this book provides you with the information and motivation to decide to address your fears, then I will be hugely gratified.

It should be noted that for some people this book alone might provide sufficient guidance for them to be able to address their phobia and free themselves from its grip. For others it may be advisable to seek the help of a professional to support you through your treatment, in the same way that you would turn to a doctor for help with a physical ailment.

There is no doubt whatsoever that phobias take a great toll on your happiness and limit what you can comfortably do in life but also, and even more damagingly, they can rob you of self-confidence and self-respect. My message to anyone with a phobia is that it must **always** be challenged. This not only emancipates you from its limitations but more importantly it promotes a sense of autonomy and personal agency which is essential for healthy living.

Always remember that a phobia is a parasite gorging off your life.

For many years I have specialized in phobias and without hesitation I can own to the fact that it is my favourite line of work within my practice. This is for two reasons. Firstly, the sheer diversity of phobias makes them a compelling and fascinating subject for study. But by far and away, the main reason why I love this field of mental health is because of the amazing job satisfaction I derive from working with clients who successfully defeat their phobias.

Phobias are very responsive to treatment

Unlike many other mental health problems, phobias can be brought under manageable control or even totally destroyed, sometimes within hours. This is a far cry from some of the medium- to long-term work which is required for other mental health issues. So the good news is that phobias are relatively easy to deal with, providing you have the correct knowledge, support and treatment plan, along with a determined and proactive attitude.

In life there are many **REAL** problems, which we all have to contend with, so my view is that we should conserve our energy to tackle those by ridding ourselves of the **UNREAL** threats, which are the hallmarks of a phobia.

Conquering a phobia not only stems the senseless drain on personal resources but will also create a tremendous confidence boost, by you having faced your fear and emerging triumphant.

Introducing the gremlin

Throughout this book I will be referring to your phobia as the gremlin, which is an imaginary mischievous creature. It seems to be a suitable nickname, since the threat, which causes your phobia, is imaginary too.

Pity the person who acquiesces to domination by the gremlin – is the dog wagging the tail or the tail wagging the dog? I urge you to take the risk to ensure that it is the former and not the latter.

Taking the **RISK** to change the status quo involves mobilizing the following:

Resilience – be determined and don't give up until you get there
Initiative – be prepared to try something new
Skills – develop the skills needed to take back control
Knowledge – acquisition of the theory to defeat your anxiety

I am on a mission to purge the population of phobias, as they are cruel fraudsters and imposters that cripple our lives and curtail our freedom to live in accordance with our choices.

What we will cover in the book

In *Section A*, I will be covering how a phobia is diagnosed and classified, along with the history of phobias, their causes and why some people are more susceptible to developing and maintaining them. We will then explore fear, anxiety, panic attacks and stress, which are all key components of a phobia.

In *Section B*, I will discuss the various available treatments for phobias and in particular I will look at Exposure Therapy, Cognitive Behavioural Therapy and the 4Rs Paradigm.

SECTION A:
Understanding Phobias

1. Phobias and Fear

What is a phobia?

A phobia is a type of fear based on a misdiagnosis of the threat

A phobia is a persistent irrational aversion to something, known as the **phobic stimulus** or **trigger**, which the sufferer feels compelled to try to avoid at all costs to prevent them from experiencing an intense anxiety response.

When unpacking this statement we can see that a phobia is an intense fear, which possesses the following characteristics:

1. It is specific to an object (e.g. statue), creature (e.g. moth), person (e.g. genius), situation (e.g. a job interview), concept (e.g. a number) or action (e.g. dancing)

2. It is irrational, excessive and unreasonable, since the feared 'something' does not pose an actual threat to the extent calculated by the sufferer; the adult sufferer is aware of this (some children are not)

3. It is usually a learned response, although some phobias may be hard-wired genetically (e.g. fear of falling or fear of loud noises)

4. Avoidance behaviour is sought by the sufferer, in that they will go to great lengths to contrive ways to not

encounter the phobic stimulus, despite it hugely inconveniencing the way that they live their life

5. The fear is persistent – in children this must be for at least six months before it can be diagnosed as a phobia

6. If the phobic stimulus is encountered the sufferer will endure intense distress.

However, avoidance is not in the long run a viable option in that it is positively injurious to the sufferer.

Avoidance is like oxygen to a phobia: it is essential to keep it alive and flourishing – while at the same time it will inevitably create a **void** in your life as you are prevented from following your own wishes and desires. The only way to be liberated to live your life fully is to confront and defeat your phobia.

A **phobia** is a:

Persistent
Hang Up or
Obstruction that
Blocks an
Individual's ability to enjoy
Autonomy

Below I have listed a dozen very common phobias, which are classified as specific phobias.

12 Common Specific Phobias

Arachnophobia	Fear of spiders
Ophidiophobia	Fear of snakes
Claustrophobia	Fear of confined spaces
Acrophobia	Fear of heights
Brontophobia	Fear of thunder
Aviaphobia	Fear of flying
Trypanophobia	Fear of injections
Mysophobia	Fear of germs
Musophobia	Fear of rats and mice
Cynophobia	Fear of dogs
Glossophobia	Fear of public speaking
Atychiphobia	Fear of failure

KEY TERM

The oldest and strongest emotion of mankind is fear.
Anonymous

Fear is a very powerful, unpleasant and distressing emotion, which we experience when we **believe** that we are at risk of serious harm, threat or impending danger.

We have this emotion for survival purposes since it will steer us away from situations that could potentially harm us. People who do not possess the ability to experience this emotion are seriously handicapped and their chances of survival are significantly diminished.

How does fear help us to survive?

Fear will activate our **fight or flight** response mechanism, making us instantly as alert and powerful as possible so that we can face the threat and fight, or run away from it. In this context fear is a protective emotion and helps to keep us safe.

Fear is activated by our beliefs

False fear and its close associate, anxiety, squeeze the life-blood out of your existence. Sadly this powerful emotion is activated by our **beliefs**, which alas are not always founded on reality. It is this false fear that we must learn to eradicate since it curtails our freedom to live our lives fully.

Fear and imagination

As a small child I recall inventing some terrifying creatures called E-cats to entertain my little brother, who adored my made-up bedtime stories. These fierce creatures lurked under the bed and could sever your arm or leg with one swift bite. Such were the powers of my imagination that I would lie immobilized and terrified in my bed in the dark, totally convinced of their existence and silently willing my parents to come up to say goodnight long after my little brother was fast asleep, he being of a more grounded constitution.

The point to be gleaned from this personal anecdote is that it did not matter if I was in **real** or **imagined** danger. My fear, based on my own overly active imagination, felt very real indeed, despite the fact that it was self-induced, and brought about the same symptoms as if the threat was genuine.

Perhaps you can remember times in the past when you have put yourself through agony due to incorrect beliefs and assumptions. Have you ever thought that you were being followed at night and in terror turned round to confront your assailant, only to discover that the noise you had heard was merely a crisp packet rustling in the wind? Though in no real danger, your body would have prepared itself just as thoroughly as if the danger were real. In chapter 7 we will look in detail at this phenomenon known as the activation of the fight or flight response.

2. Types of Phobia

Classification of phobias

DSM-IV

Phobias are divided into various categories depending on the level of sophistication and complexity of the classification system. The most commonly used classification system is taken from the *Diagnostic and Statistical Manual of Mental Disorders, Fourth Edition*, commonly referred to as the **DSM-IV**. In this system, phobias are allocated to three groups, namely social phobias, specific phobias and Agoraphobia. The specific phobia group is further broken down into five groups these being, ***animal, blood-injection-injury, situational, natural environment** and **other***. For our purpose in this practical guide, we will follow the **DSM-IV** classification system on the whole. However, we will break down the category referred to as 'other' into ***people*** and ***objects***. *We will also* refer to the 'blood-injection-injury' category as ***medical/body-based phobias***. The specific phobias will be referred to as **simple** phobias and Agoraphobia and social phobias will be termed **complex** phobias:

Simple phobias *(equivalent to the DSM-IV specific phobias)*

Simple phobias are grouped together under the following category headings, and in each category you will find a brief case study to illustrate a particular phobia.

1. **Animal phobias** e.g. fear of bees, rats, jellyfish, sharks, eels, birds, wasps, lice, rabbits, cows, spiders, snakes, lizards, crabs, bats, frogs, horses, dogs, monkeys, pigs, slugs, crocodiles, hamsters or cats.

Sciurophobia
Fear of Squirrels

Darcy developed a fear of squirrels when, aged ten, a glis glis, which is an edible dormouse, had managed to get inside of his bedroom. The glis glis knocked over an ornament on his bedside locker, which startled Darcy. The glis glis did not seem to know how to find its way out of the room and ran amok whilst Darcy sat frozen to the spot in terror. Darcy, unsurprisingly, developed a fear of glis glis, which also extended to a fear of squirrels due to their similarity in appearance.

As a result of this experience Darcy would not go into the garden unless his dog went out first, reasoning that the dog's presence would deter either of these creatures. He also flatly refused to go on any school trips which involved walking in the woods, parks or anywhere he felt might be a habitat for a squirrel or a glis glis.

---

2. **Medical/body-based phobias** e.g. fear of sleep, death, suffocating, choking, being cold or hot, being diseased, being anaesthetized, being injured, being sick, receiving

stitches, going to hospital, giving birth, having an x-ray or operation, inoculation, blood transfusion.

Tokophobia

Fear of Giving Birth

Sunita developed a fear of giving birth when as a small child she watched a film in which the heroine went through considerable agonies before succumbing to death in childbirth. The fear was further compounded when in her early teens she heard her elder sister scream out in pain whilst giving birth to her first child.

Sunita felt both ashamed and embarrassed by her fear and did not disclose this to her family. Having sabotaged all her romantic relationships as a young adult, Sunita eventually met a partner with whom she wanted to share the rest of her life. Recognizing that her boyfriend wanted a family she eventually decided that she needed to address this fear and sought help.

---

3. **Situational/action phobias** e.g. fear of travelling through a tunnel, crossing a bridge, driving on a motorway, flying in turbulence, climbing a ladder, travelling on the Underground, sailing on the sea, diving off a board, skiing down a mountain or walking by a canal.

Subterrenus-Siderodromophobia

Fear of travelling on the Underground

Harry had recently broken up with his girlfriend, whom he had been dating for three years, whilst they were at university together. She had decided to take a job abroad and felt that they should end their relationship. Harry had struggled through his finals due to suffering from glandular fever, which was not diagnosed until he visited his doctor at the end of his exams. Harry had not done as well as expected in his exams on account of feeling too exhausted to study.

One day, whilst recovering from his illness, he returned home from a hospital check-up by tube train. The train stopped in a tunnel for a considerable amount of time as a consequence of a signal problem. During this time Harry started to panic and felt that he must get off the train since he felt he was unable to catch his breath. He became increasingly distressed and was convinced that he was going to suffocate. People around him were very kind and supportive but Harry felt absolutely desperate.

When the train eventually continued its journey, Harry got off at the very next stop and called his parents to come and collect him. For two years Harry flatly refused to travel by tube train. Harry was offered an interview in Manchester for a job that he was anxious to get. To Harry's dismay the minute he boarded the overland train to Manchester he was overwhelmed with panic and had to get off immediately. At this point he realized that he needed to deal with his fear since it had expanded to a fear of trains as well as a fear of the Underground.

4. **Natural environment phobias** e.g. fear of snow, heights, trees, dirt, earthquakes, avalanches, sounds, sunlight, echoes, landslides, dust, fog, clouds, thunder, the dark, volcanoes, water, fire, cyclones, rocks meteorites, vapour, shadows, sand, lightening, waves, plants, storms, forests, hailstones rivers, ice, mist, swamps, quicksand, mountains.

Aquaphobia
Fear of Water

Dionny was Ariel's best man and attended his stag weekend in Riga. The boys stayed in a very luxurious hotel in Latvia's capital. After dining out, the group returned to the hotel and ordered a nightcap. One drink led to another and very soon the party became more and more inebriated.

Patrick then rallied the group to bomb into the swimming pool fully clothed. Dionny led the charge and leapt into the pool, but before he surfaced he felt the impact of a heavy blow from the feet of another member of the group, which forced him back under the water. He lost his bearings, but eventually managed to make his way to the surface, only to be dunked under again by another member of the party who was indulging in a bit of horseplay.

Stunned, weak and disorientated, Dionny was eventually pulled out of the pool by Ellis, who had recognized that he was in grave danger. As a result of this unfortunate experience Dionny, a previously keen and competent swimmer, developed an absolute terror of water, which prevented him from swimming, sailing and waterskiing, all pursuits which he had previously enjoyed.

---

5. **People phobias** e.g. fear of dentists, women, doctors, teachers, clowns, strangers, people in wheelchairs, men, elderly people, obese people, priests, teenagers, transvestites; people with disfigurements, amputations, learning difficulties, anorexia; people who are bald, hirsute, sweaty, greedy, make noises when eating.

Androphobia
Fear of Men

Afia had been sent from Africa to Scotland to stay with her maternal aunt aged eleven. For the journey she had been put in the charge of Daudi, a 30-year-old friend of Afia's eldest brother, who took great delight in filling poor Afia's head with all sorts of nonsense about what she would encounter when she reached her destination.

Daudi's intention was to amuse himself by witnessing Afia's incredulity about the wild animals, cannibalism and horrific rituals which she was about to meet once she arrived in the UK. Although he considered his amusement as just harmless teasing, Afia, already distressed by leaving her family behind, was totally traumatized by what she had been told. On arriving in England Afia became very clingy towards her aunt and would scream if her uncle tried to interact with her. Afia developed a total mistrust and fear of men and was unable to tolerate male teachers or even the company of any males connected with her aunt's family. It was not until Afia was a young woman that she disclosed her experience to a close girl friend who urged her to seek help.

6. **Object and concept phobias** e.g. dolls, musical instruments, chalk, time, eternity, angles, foods, telephones, colours, scales, towers, cages, poltergeists, velour, beds, blinds, gates, paper, feathers, gas cookers, tractors, nylon, shelves, sandpaper, glue, disinfectant, chimneys, soap, fans, escalators, dustbins, nightmares, failure.

Atychiphobia
Fear of Failure
Li Na was the middle child of an academically gifted Chinese family. Li Na attended the same school as her elder siblings but constantly

struggled to achieve the same high standards as her sisters. Her teachers accused her of being lazy and not trying since there was clearly no lack of brains and ability within her family. Li Na did her best and studied far harder than her sisters but never achieved results that were anything other than average.

Frustrated and upset by her alleged lack of concentration and effort, Li Na came to dread all class tests and annual exams. As a way of self-protection she would contrive all manner of excuses as to why she was unable to go to school and fabricated a range of symptoms to prevent her attendance. The problem was further exacerbated when Li Na's younger sister joined the school and rapidly rose to the top of her year group.

Li Na felt that she was a total disappointment to her parents and dreaded any activity that compounded this sense of failure. Soon she refused to attend sports and speech days and avoided any situations where she was required to sit an exam. A pattern of playing truant became established and Li Na became defiant and rebellious.

On leaving school at the earliest opportunity, Li Na took a job in a local hotel, helping in the kitchen. The head chef swiftly came to rely on Li Na who was quick to learn and had a natural aptitude for cooking. Keen to encourage his protégé's advancement, he suggested that she take various qualifications, which would entitle her to a higher salary and greater job opportunities. Li Na saw that he was determined that she should progress further and instantly handed in her notice since the thought of examinations made her feel panicky.

This pattern of gaining recognition by her employer leading to talk of further qualifications and Li Na's subsequent resignations repeated itself several times more before Li Na, now in her late twenties, decided to confront her fear of failure.

Complex phobias

This category, as the name implies, is made up of fears, which are more complex in that they cover a variety of situations, occasions and circumstances and can therefore be generally much more debilitating for the sufferer. **Social phobias** and **Agoraphobia** are included in this group.

Since complex phobias are so prolific in Western society, I think that it is important that we look at them in some detail in the following chapters.

Multiple phobias

It is important to note that just as some people have several physical disorders concurrently, the same may be the case with people having several phobias at one time. Woody Allen is a striking example of this phenomenon and is often described as being **Panophobic**, which means a fear of everything. Although strictly speaking this descriptor is an exaggeration, the list below, which is not comprehensive, does demonstrate that his fears are quite extensive. As well as having a fear of lifts and tunnels he is also reported as having:

Insectophobic	Fear of insects
Acrophobic	Fear of heights
Cynophobic	Fear of animals
Enochlophobic	Fear of crowds
Claustrophobic	Fear of enclosed spaces
Carcinophobic	Fear of cancer
Chromophobic	Fear of bright colours
Arachibutyrophobic	Fear of peanut butter sticking to the mouth

3. Social Phobias

Damage to social life

Social phobias can amount to a fear of attending social functions such as weddings, funerals, cocktail parties, bar mitzvahs, stag parties or conferences. In fact any situation in which the individual feels that they may be judged and found wanting, thus risking humiliation and embarrassment, will be problematic for them.

In the USA it is believed to be the third most common mental health disorder, affecting up to 12 per cent of the population. For some people the circumstances of the social phobia may be relatively contained but for others it can blight every aspect of their life, particularly if it causes them to be unable to have a social life.

Damage to education and career

Social phobia typically develops in a young person during their teenage years when their level of self-consciousness tends to be particularly acute. Negative feedback from parents, peers and teachers can cause considerable damage to an adolescent who is already contending with other difficulties.

During this life stage, young people are exposed to a wider range of social situations as they move towards adulthood, which in turn provokes greater anxiety as they test out new behaviours and wonder about other people's expectations. Along with this, they are also negotiating physical and hormonal changes whilst struggling with questions concerning their identity.

Parents are fully aware of the potential volatility of a teenage child who will tend to inflate negative feedback and discount the positive. Later on in the book we will look at this cognitive distortion known as 'filtering', a form of selective thinking which is particularly prevalent within this age group.

As well as deterring people from taking part in social functions, social phobias prevent people from being able to participate in general everyday activities, such as attending school or going to work. This, as you can imagine, carries serious consequences in terms of educational achievement and financial potential, which further reduces the individual's level of confidence.

Fear of being judged

People with social phobias may be overly self-critical and lack confidence in the way that they speak, walk, dress, eat or write, among other difficulties. To someone with these dispositions, making a speech, walking into an exhibition, dressing for a gala evening, dining in a restaurant or having to sign a contract can be a gruelling and petrifying experience which they will do all in their power to avoid.

Any situation where the sufferer feels that another will evaluate their performance will cause immense anxiety. If they need to sign a cheque, their hand would probably

28

shake uncontrollably as a result of the anxiety symptoms and hence their embarrassment and humiliation would be confirmed, causing a vicious cycle to become established.

Impact of social phobia is more debilitating

As you can appreciate, social phobias are much more complex than simple phobias. We can try to avoid, for example, snakes or travelling by rail, but it is extremely difficult to totally avoid coming into contact with other people. Our basic human need for attention, relationships, love and support would not be met if we avoided all human interaction

Sadly, people suffering from social phobias are very reticent about seeking help since this involves presenting themselves in front of another individual, thus risking further judgement. Generally less than 20 per cent of sufferers seek treatment, despite the devastating impact this phobia has upon their lives.

The anxiety caused by social phobia is not only difficult to bear, but the exclusion from fully participating in life and being able to enjoy fulfilling relationships can often lead to depression. Social phobia and depression frequently go hand in hand with drug and alcohol abuse, which is partaken in to mitigate the acute anxiety generated by social interaction.

People with social phobias do their best to avoid social interactions whenever possible. They are convinced that what they have to say will be perceived as stupid or boring. They endeavour to remain in the background and avoid eye contact rather than confirm their worst fears, which is to be humiliated or rejected.

From an evolutionary point of view, rejection from the group was like a death sentence since early man could not survive in isolation. Living in a hostile environment with predators ready to pounce on a sleeping human, cavemen took turns to watch over the group so that if any threat presented itself they would be able to alert the others and flee or fight.

It is believed that the fear of public speaking, which affects a large number of the population, derives from this need for acceptance by the group in order to survive. Today, if we make a hash of a speech the consequences are, at worst, the loss of employment but much more likely it will just result in humiliation and embarrassment. Yet many people regard performing in front of a large group of their peers as being something akin to facing a firing squad. Expressions like, 'I wanted the ground to open up and swallow me' reflect the depth of our shame and pain when we fall short of others' expectations.

Anya came to England aged six as a result of her family being persecuted in their homeland, Turkey. Anya joined her school shortly after the Easter holidays, and due to her inability to speak English was put into a class of five-year-olds. The children were given a simple exercise in which they had to pair a picture on a chart with the matching word. The children had been working on these words during the previous term and the exercise had been set as a reminder to consolidate the previous learning.

In turn the children got up and selected a word and accurately matched it with its corresponding picture. When Anya's turn arrived she understood what she had to do but had no idea which word matched which picture. She picked up a word and stood transfixed in front of the chart despite the teacher's attempt to guide her towards the correct picture. The children were naturally inquisitive about their new classmate and stared relentlessly at Anya.

Shy, embarrassed and acutely aware of the unwanted attention she was receiving, Anya felt overwhelmed in the spotlight. She did not understand what the other children were saying as the seconds ticked by, but she did comprehend their laughter. She stood immobilized to the spot, tears streaming down her face, until the teacher gently led her away to the staff room.

This experience left Anya feeling very vulnerable and she avoided the other children during the breaks and became a lonely, solitary figure in the schoolyard. Anya convinced herself that social isolation was preferable to risking another unbearable situation like the one she had experienced in the classroom. She told herself that she **could not tolerate** further humiliation.

The other children learned to ignore her as any overtures of friendship were met with silence and awkwardness, indeed she appeared to the other children as stand-offish and remote. This further confirmed Anya's skewed thinking that she was boring and unacceptable to the other children.

Anya's vulnerability and insecurity made her reluctant to ever venture an opinion in class despite the fact that her written work, over the years, revealed that she was an exceptionally able student. Anya's terror of courting ridicule or rejection led her to a very lonely existence. She would **catastrophize** the consequences of speaking out and believed that being anything other than silent and almost invisible would just result in jeers from her classmates.

The other children's parents stopped inviting her to parties and outings since all invitations were politely declined by Anya's parents. Anya simply refused to attend anything other than school and told her parents that the other children laughed at her funny accent and only sought her company so that they could poke fun at her. Anya's mother, who had also been painfully shy as a child, swiftly acquiesced to the situation and allowed Anya to lead a hermit-like existence when not at school.

Naturally, due to having little experience of social inter-action, Anya chose to become increasingly reclusive as she grew up and found solace and company in her books and studies. Not surprisingly Anya, being a gifted and hardwork-ing student, excelled in her exams and won a scholarship to a leading university. Her parents were thrilled with her achievement and Anya accepted the opportunity mainly to please them. She believed that she would be able to continue with her education as before by sitting mutely at the back of the class offering no eye contact or verbal communication with her tutors or peers.

Anya soon learned that the silent absorption of knowledge alone was not acceptable at this institution. She was expected to debate and discuss, with fellow students, arguments and opinions within intimate tutorial settings. Within this context there was no opportunity to remain invisible and silent if she was to succeed. Anya struggled desperately with the simplest of conversations when a fellow student made an overture of friendship. Her clumsiness and inability to connect with other people confirmed her predictions and became a **self-fulfilling prophecy**.

The most basic social interaction felt excruciatingly embarrassing due to her lack of experience of social intercourse. Furthermore, Anya engaged in the cognitive distortion known as **mind-reading** where she persuaded herself that she knew what her peers thought of her and needless to say this was not complimentary.

Anya dreaded her timetabled tutorials with a passion and would blush to the roots the moment she entered the room. Eventually the anxiety symptoms became so acute that she was unable to sleep the night before a tutorial. She would get up in the morning exhausted and weary, unable to hold down any food, due to the incessant churning of her stomach.

Anya resorted to drinking alcohol to dull the symptoms and to give her Dutch courage to enable her to turn up to the tutorials. Her increased self-focus made her acutely aware of her symptoms and she became convinced that these would be highly visible to her peers and tutors and they would notice that she was shaking and trembling.

Needless to say this **safety behaviour** of drinking did not help the situation, since when she found the courage to speak she was not able to formulate cogent arguments as a result of her intoxication. This then served to further compound her deeply held belief that she was no good in social situations.

Anya received several warnings about her alcohol abuse and scored low marks for her lack of contribution and participation within group projects. This sadly led to her eventual dismissal from the university.

Too ashamed to return home, Anya remained in her university accommodation for a further three weeks and woefully neglected to feed herself properly.

The humiliation and perceived disgrace resulting from this failure caused Anya to slide into a deep depression. Eventually her plight was discovered and her parents on learning about the situation were distraught and mortified to find out how Anya's social phobia had cost their beloved daughter not only a promising future but her health too.

On her return home, Anya's parent's encouraged her to accept immediate treatment from the GP, which initially consisted of a course of antidepressants. Once Anya became more stable she agreed to meet with a therapist who offered her **cognitive behavioural therapy** (**CBT**). (We will be looking at this form of treatment in chapter 13.) By means of this therapy, Anya slowly learned to challenge her fear of social situations without needing to resort to crutches, such as alcohol.

Gradually, by putting herself into her feared situations, Anya gained concrete proof that she wasn't perceived as boring, weird or alien, ideas she had incubated since she was six years old. Urged on by her increasing confidence, Anya, a natural student, devoured self-help books on social anxiety. She further hastened her recovery by applying a raft of relaxation techniques, which she acquired through her reading.

I am happy to report that Anya now has a doctorate, a fulfilling career and a happy family life with her husband Antoine. Had she not found the courage to tackle her social phobia it would have been a very different story.

When analysing Anya's development of a social phobia it is easy to see that it was initially triggered by a painful **personal experience**. You can imagine the trauma experienced by a bright young child, unable to communicate, uprooted from her home and country to find herself humiliated in front of a group of younger children.

Anya's **internal belief** that she would appear as strange and alien to the other children endorsed her need to avoid social interactions. This **avoidance** meant that she was denied the opportunity to develop social skills and so her awkwardness and gaucheness became a **self-fulfilling prophecy**; that she was not acceptable in social groups.

As the years went by the gap between Anya's social skills and those expected for her age became more and more pronounced, which in turn racked up the volume of her **internal anxiety**. This gave her the further impetus to avoid more and more opportunities to interact with others and thus the gulf became increasingly wider and seemingly insurmountable.

With the now concrete evidence of her own ineptitude in social situations before her, it was easy for Anya to maintain her phobia. It was not until Anya reached a crisis point and was compelled to accept help and support that the phobia was eventually confronted and challenged.

By accepting CBT, Anya was able to challenge her negative cognitive distortions, such as **mind-reading**, **personalizing**, **filtering, catastrophizing** and **intolerant thinking**. (We will cover these terms in more detail in chapter 14.) The less she brainwashed herself that everyone didn't like her or found her stupid, the less she blushed and sweated, since her anxiety level was lower. This in turn gave her more confidence to scrutinize the evidence and she discovered that people were not judging her negatively.

As her self-esteem grew, Anya's negative, defensive body language changed and people found her more welcoming and approachable. A virtuous cycle displaced the vicious cycle as she became increasingly comfortable in her own skin and people felt more drawn to her company.

In time, friendships blossomed and Anya became more adventurous as her self-confidence soared. As a result of her treatment she became much more pragmatic and balanced and accepted the fact that in life we can't expect to meet everyone's expectations and that that is OK. Eventually Anya felt sufficiently secure within herself to resume her studies, and the rest, as they say, is history.

4. Agoraphobia

I have left discussion of this phobia to the last since it is, without argument, the most debilitating phobia of all. Someone with a full-blown social phobia can find that his or her life is radically curtailed but at least can still derive some pleasure from being on their own on a beautiful desert island. For someone with full-blown agoraphobia there can sometimes be no peace for them whatsoever. The daily terror of facing an unexpected panic attack dogs their every thought and they become terrified of their own shadow.

Agoraphobia, which directly translates as a fear of the marketplace, is the term applied to people who, fearing the possibility of a panic attack, find being in unfamiliar territory a terrifying experience. This is largely down to the fact that they need to feel confident about their means of escape and certainty of support should they feel endangered in any way. Within unfamiliar territory their sense of control is significantly diminished so they tend to avoid these environments at all costs.

Naturally, there are varying degrees of agoraphobia, with some people limited to being comfortable only within their own village or town, to those who cannot venture beyond a tiny physical area such as their bedroom. It is believed that agoraphobia accounts for over 50 per cent of phobias in Western civilization. Compounding this alarming statistic is the fact that agoraphobia can wreak total havoc within an individual's life, causing astounding personal and financial costs to the sufferer and their dependents.

For people suffering from agoraphobia, visits to shopping malls, cinemas, theatres, synagogues, football stadiums, concerts, theme parks, mosques and zoos can prove overwhelmingly threatening. In short, any place that runs the risk of having crowds and an unclear view of potential escape exits become anathema to them and they gradually confine themselves to their home territory.

Sadly, even within their own houses, some of these sufferers feel so insecure that they need to have a companion with them at all times. The net result is that they lead their lives as if they were under house arrest, not daring to step over the boundary of their front door. It is easy to envisage the psychological toll this has on an individual's self-confidence and sense of autonomy.

Suffering from agoraphobia can bar people from travelling and prevent them from being able to support their families, since they can become incapable of holding down gainful employment. It can also severely compromise their ability to enjoy meaningful personal relationships, since significant others in their life seldom welcome having their lives circumscribed within such narrow limits. Simple things like enjoying a pub lunch with friends or going on a family holiday become totally impossible for someone suffering from agoraphobia and many partners struggle to acquiesce to this level of incarceration.

Agoraphobia is most common in women, up to twice as prevalent as in men, and tends to develop between the ages of 20 and 40. For a variety of reasons people tend to soldier on with this difficult burden for a decade before admitting that they need professional help. It is often at the point when they have lost a great deal, in terms of relationships, employment and self-respect, that people in desperation recognize that they can no longer function in this manner.

Needless to say, agoraphobia and depression are close bedfellows since living in the shadow of a potential panic attack is gruelling and exhausting, to say the least, and would rob any life of joy. Try to picture a life where the simplest daily routines are thwarted by a never-ending fear that you might have a panic attack.

Would you dare to drive your children to school, invite friends to supper or volunteer to join a local team if you believed that at any moment you could be fighting for every breath with your heart pounding and your body shaking uncontrollably?

Because the symptoms experienced in a panic attack – which we will talk about in more detail later – can emulate real physical disorders such as cardiac arrest, people, although aware that a panic attack is not dangerous, never cease to wonder if this time it might not be just a panic attack but a real heart attack. As a consequence of this, sufferers are not only fearful about their own lives but are reluctant to put others in danger too. I think that you can easily get the picture of how a sufferer's life can become narrower and narrower.

Agoraphobia

Andrew was a successful, high-flying hedge fund manager whose career had shot to great heights before he reached 35 years of age. This meteoric rise was not merely the result of serendipitous agents but was backed up by a gruelling regime of toil and graft. It is fair to say that Andrew burnt the candle at both ends, leaving for the office at five each morning and seldom returning before ten in the evening.

The weekends were merely an extension of Andrew's working week, consisting of incessant networking, work preparation and entertaining. His young family saw very little of him. By day, Andrew was either locked away in his study, on the telephone arranging meetings or out and about on the golf course schmoozing potential clients. In the evening he would return late from the restaurant, exhausted and triumphant, having closed further deals or forged promising new contacts.

Despite the constant warnings from friends and family that he needed to let up a bit and take some time out to relax, Andrew insisted on continuing at this manic rate. Even a few health scares and the stern words of his GP did not deter Andrew from keeping up the cracking pace which he had set for himself. He was determined to achieve his financial goal and be able to retire, in luxury, at the age of 40 and nothing was going to stop him.

Although everyone had warned Andrew that his current lifestyle was not sustainable, it was not until he experienced a panic attack that Andrew was forced to heed the advice which he had so freely disregarded. Whilst attending a conference in Geneva, Andrew suddenly felt very strange and started to feel frightened and panicky. Pinned between two colleagues in the middle of the auditorium he experienced an urgent need to get out of the room. He felt that he was fighting to breathe, his stomach was uncomfortable and a nauseous sensation pervaded every cell in his body.

The guest speaker had just begun his speech and Andrew felt detached and distant from everything, but was still acutely aware of the disruption he would cause if he tried to leave his seat at this point. Beads of perspiration sprung up on his forehead and his hands began to shake uncontrollably. Looking around in desperation for a way out everything took on a surreal quality. He was conscious of the laughter echoing from the hall as the keynote speaker cracked jokes and received volleys of applause and 'hear hears' from the audience, but what was actually being said he could not decipher.

One of Andrew's colleagues turned to him to acknowledge the hilarity of the speaker's wisecracks only to notice his pallid and ashen face. Andrew's colleague, realizing that he was unwell, swiftly took action and Andrew was removed instantly and publicly from the auditorium. A doctor was called and it was agreed that he be sent immediately to the University Hospital Geneva, where he received a comprehensive check-up in the Medical Center.

The Swiss doctor assured Andrew that there was no evidence of a physiological problem and that his recent experience bore all the hallmarks of a panic attack. The doctor recommended that he rest for a few days and then return to England and make an appointment to see his GP. Embarrassed by the episode, Andrew told his colleagues that he had suffered from food poisoning and his firm unquestioningly accepted this ruse.

Andrew had been so convincing in his cover-up of the panic attack that he actually believed his own rhetoric and did not seek medical help or ease up on his return to England. Two days after his return Andrew endured a similar experience whilst entertaining some contacts over dinner in his favourite restaurant. Recognizing the symptoms, Andrew immediately excused himself and, much to the consternation of his guests, rapidly left the room and did not return. On reaching the pavement outside he hailed a taxi and, shaking in terror, leapt inside.

Once safely ensconced in the taxi, the symptoms started to abate and he was able to draw his breath more easily and the nauseous feeling started to subside. On arriving home uncharacteristically early, Andrew admitted to his wife that he was feeling under the weather and would be taking some time out from work. The next day he called the office and informed them that he had damaged his back and would therefore be running things from home for the next few weeks.

Sadly, the work of a hedge fund manager does not lend itself to working from home on a permanent basis, but the thought of returning to the office instantly brought on anxiety symptoms. Andrew made several attempts to return to work but felt compelled to return home before reaching the office car park. The thought of experiencing another panic attack remained a constant fixture in his mind and served to exacerbate his ongoing anxiety.

Much to Andrew and his family's consternation, he started to become distressed about doing errands close to home after experiencing a full-blown panic attack whilst filling up his car with petrol at the local garage. On this occasion the panic attack had been so overwhelming that Andrew was convinced that he was having a heart attack and was about to die. Medics were called to the forecourt and Andrew was taken to hospital by ambulance where he was admitted for an overnight stay and a full battery of tests.

The panic attacks after this last incident became increasingly regular, making Andrew reluctant to leave the safety of his own home. In short, Andrew's world became smaller and smaller and he only dared venture out when accompanied by his wife, Morgan.

The constant feeling of vulnerability impacted not only on Andrew's working life but also took its toll in other ways. As his appetite diminished, his alcohol consumption increased. He became lethargic and listless and took no interest in his family life, being totally consumed by his problems.

After several months, Andrew was contacted by his firm's HR department seeking clarification of his current state of health. It was at this juncture that Andrew realized that the problem was not going away on its own and in fact was becoming increasingly severe. He disclosed the real cause of his absence from the office and offered to hand in his resignation. His employer was very understanding and encouraged Andrew to contact the employee assistance programme. Within days Andrew underwent a full physical and psychological assessment.

This was followed by a course of treatment in which Andrew was taught anxiety management techniques, how to identify the situations that triggered his anxiety and how to use relaxation exercises. With the help of a clinical psychologist, Andrew worked through a series of feared situations until he eventually felt confident enough to return to his work. (This is known as **exposure therapy**, which we will be covering in chapter 11.)

On his return to work, four months later, Andrew vowed to keep his work/life balance within saner proportions. He now takes time for relaxation and sleep, and plays a much more active role in family life. The agoraphobic episode in his life was a salutary experience, which caused Andrew to reorder his priorities. Andrew is the first to recognize how fortunate he had been in getting help so swiftly to address his agoraphobia before it took its toll on his marriage and livelihood.

From this case study we can see that sometimes phobias appear to come out of the blue and for no apparent reason. However, on reflection we can see that there was a reason, since Andrew had ignored health warnings and allowed himself to operate under a relentless regime of very high stress levels.

The outcome of excessive stress can be manifested physically in some people, causing migraines, ulcers or irritable bowel syndrome, for example. Others are more predisposed to developing mental health problems such as acquiring a phobia or having what we term a nervous breakdown.

The development of a phobia is often the body's way of saying 'enough is enough' and forcing us to slow down. In Andrew's case, his stress was shown on both a physical and psychological level.

Everyone has different tolerance levels with regards to handling stress, along with different degrees of physical or psychological susceptibility relating to how they react to excessive stress. It is important that we do not ignore the signals which our body sends out and that we strive to maintain a healthy, balanced lifestyle.

5. Phobias –
History, Targets and Causes

The history of phobias

Phobias have been around for a very long time. The earliest reference to them was by Hippocrates in the fourth century BC, although the name 'phobia' was not coined until much later. The term was fashioned after a Greek god known as Phobus, whose horrifying countenance was used to scare the enemy. Celsus, a Roman doctor, allegedly described a patient in the advanced stages of rabies being terrified of water and claimed that he was 'hydrophobic' and thus the term came into use. Modern usage of the term was not until 1786 when a phobia was defined as:

A fear of an imaginary evil, or an undue fear of a real one.
Oxford English Dictionary

Who can get a phobia?

The simple answer to this question is that **anyone** can become the target for a phobia. Phobias show no respect for age, gender, socio-economic class, race, culture, wealth, talent, education or any other variable you can think of. However, as we shall see later, there are certain factors which will increase your risk of acquiring a phobia. If you have a phobia, you are far from alone, as the list of celebrities below amply illustrates.

25 famous people who reportedly suffer from phobias

Madonna
Fear of thunder (Brontophobia)

David Beckham
Fear of messiness (Ataxophobia)

Pamela Anderson
Fear of her own reflection (Eisoptrophobia)

Kelly Osbourne
Fear of being touched (Haphophobia)

Britney Spears
Fear of lizards (Herpetophobia)

Johnny Depp
Fear of clowns (Coulrophobia)

Scarlet Johansson
Fear of birds (Ornithophobia)

Nicole Kidman
Fear of butterflies (Lepidoterophobia)

Christina Ricci
Fear of plants (Botanophobia)

Oprah Winfrey
Fear of chewing gum (Chiclephobia)

Robert Pattinson
Fear of horses (Equinophobia)

Megan Fox
Fear of paper (Papyrophobia)

Helen Mirren
Fear of childbirth (Tokophobia)

Andy Roddick
Fear of rabbits (Leporiphobia)

Alfred Hitchcock
Fear of eggs (Ovaphobia)

Orlando Bloom
Fear of pigs (Swinophobia)

Cameron Diaz
Fear of doorknobs (Ostiumtractophobia)

Robert de Niro
Fear of dentistry (Odontophobia)

Lyle Lovett
Fear of cows (Taurophobia)

Kylie Minogue
Fear of coat hangers (Tunicamadesculaphobia)

Keanu Reeves
Fear of the dark (Nyctophobia)

Tyra Banks
Fear of dolphins (Delphiniphobia)

Muhammad Ali
Fear of flying (Aviophobia)

Woody Allen
Fear of bright colours (Chromophobia)

Damian Lillard
Fear of statues (Automatophobia)

Cheryl Cole
Fear of cotton wool (Bambakomallophobia)

How are phobias acquired?

There are a number of ways in which you can acquire a phobia.

1. Frightening personal experience – trauma

Someone may have had a very unpleasant personal experience, such as being stung by a jellyfish or bucked off a horse. Quite naturally this will cause them to be wary of these animals and they could easily develop a phobia as a consequence. This is particularly the case if they allow a considerable amount of time to elapse before resuming their activities of swimming in the sea or riding. We even have an expression, 'if you fall off a horse, get right back on', which advocates a swift return to an activity if we have had a traumatic experience so as to pre-empt the possibility of **avoidance** setting in.

Sometimes the trauma may be indirect and has happened to someone else, but nonetheless it can lead to vicarious traumatization. Watching a cousin choking on a salmon bone could be a terrifying experience for a young child and if not addressed, can result in a lifelong fear of consuming all types of fish.

Fasciaephobia

Fear of Shelves

At the age of six and a half, Mickey had been woken up during the night when the small shelf above his bed had come loose. The shelf did not actually hit him but the loud noise, which awoke him from a deep sleep, along with the avalanche of soft toys that fell on his head, terrified him.

As a consequence of this experience Mickey developed a fear of shelves. No amount of explaining or soothing from his parents would convince the traumatized little boy that shelves were relatively harmless and that this had been a freak event. Mickey's parents at last gave in to him and removed all the other shelves in his bedroom, after enduring several nights of his sobbing and refusing to sleep there.

As Mickey grew up he did everything in his power to avoid coming too close to a shelf. As you can imagine this phobia was quite debilitating since even a simple shopping expedition to the local store was something that Mickey would be wary about.

---

2. Modelling – observational learning

Copying someone else's behaviour is another way in which phobias can develop. This is the way that we learn positive skills like knowing how to use our knife and fork at the table or how to do Scottish dancing. Sadly, observational learning or modelling can work in a negative way too.

This can happen when we witness someone else's intense fear, such as a grandparent who shrieks at the sight of a bat. Children are particularly prone to developing a phobia in this manner since they have less experience to draw upon and therefore will accept it as normal to be afraid of bats.

Lachanophobia
Fear of Vegetables
Marvin, aged two and a half, was enjoying a family picnic when suddenly his mother screamed and then proceeded to gag. She stuck her fingers down her throat in between screeching and tried to retch up her meal. Marvin was too young to comprehend his mother's bizarre behaviour. The cause of the episode was the sight of half a slug on Marvin's mother's plate and her not unreasonable assumption that she had inadvertently consumed the other half. Consequently, Marvin developed an acute phobia of all vegetables of a green variety.

Below is a personal example which shows how easily a phobia can develop or be averted through observational learning.

Ophidiophobia
Fear of Snakes
On one occasion my children had been given a guided tour of the Emperor Valley Zoo in Trinidad as a birthday treat. The delightful zookeeper could see that my four-year-old son was having a whale of

a time, holding spiders in his hand and allowing snakes to crawl up and down his t-shirt and peep out through the armholes. My three-year-old daughter looked less sanguine to say the least.

Charlo, the zookeeper, had picked up on the fact that she looked uneasy and went to a small pen and took out a writhing ball of baby mapapi snakes. He spoke to my daughter and explained that they were only babies so she must hold the ball firmly so that the baby snakes felt secure and safe. Alas, she was having none of it and promptly dropped the ball of snakes that he had handed to her.

Noticing that she looked on the verge of tears, and without missing a beat, Charlo gently scooped up the baby snakes and moulded them back into a ball. He then said to my daughter, 'Look, Mummy wants to hold them', while passing them over to me with a look that said 'don't you dare let your daughter down'.

Now I have to own that I was not overly big on snakes but I did have the wit to understand the potential consequences of my refusal to hold them. I pinned on my face my brightest smile and took the writhing ball while muttering all sorts of nonsense about how cute and sweet they looked and how tickly they felt when they wriggled in my hands. Within seconds my daughter reached out for them stating that she wanted a turn holding them because she wanted to feel what they were like when they wriggled.

My children continued to enjoy the rest of the visit but I was noticeably absent when it came to feeding live rats to the big snakes. There is after all a limit to maternal duties and in my book watching this spectacle was a bridge too far!

---

3. Misunderstanding

An incorrect interpretation of the facts is another cause of phobia development and this again is particularly prevalent in children. For example a number of children find clowns or Punch and Judy shows to be terrifying on account of the hideous, garish faces which they, not unsurprisingly, equate with evil and danger.

There are considerable numbers of young children who become **Samhainophobic**, which is a fear of Halloween as a result of finding the macabre costumes positively scary. The incidence of **Wiccaphobia** and **Phasomophobia**, which are the fear of witches and ghosts respectively, are also attributed in large part to this celebration.

Even bonfire night can be terrifying for a small child who witnesses the practice of burning an effigy on the bonfire. Despite being told that the figure is not real, the lifelike characteristics of some masks can cause a small child to become confused and distressed.

Misunderstandings are even common in adults. The natural creaking of a house during the night, caused by changes in temperature, may be construed by those of a more lively imagination as a sign that it is haunted. This may result in them having to go to the inconvenience and expense of moving since their fear makes living in the house intolerable.

Ambulothanatophobia
Fear of Zombies

Marcus and Molly were having a 'Ghoulies, Zombies and Ghosties' fancy dress party to celebrate their tenth wedding anniversary when their three-year-old daughter, Constance, was awoken by the noise. She made her way down the stairs and popped her head round the living room door calling out for her mother. On seeing the macabre collection of dancers she not unnaturally started to scream and bawl.

On witnessing the child's terror, several of the dressed-up revellers rushed forward to calm Constance down, which only served to inflame her hysterics further. Marcus, on hearing Constance's demonic screams, rushed from the kitchen and picked her up saying, 'You're OK, Daddy's here.' Dressed as a headless horseman, Marcus' soothing words were wasted on poor Constance as she ramped up the decibel level of her screams.

It was not until her uncle had the wit to remove his werewolf mask that Constance's distress plateaued, by which time Molly had worked herself free from the majority of her mummy outfit and was able to comfort her distraught daughter. It was not an easy task to convince a petrified three-year-old that what she was seeing was not real but just adults dressing up for fun!

---

4. Indoctrination

A considerable number of people develop a fear of something as a result of the constant brainwashing which they receive from significant others. For example, children who have been overly warned about 'stranger danger' can become petrified in the presence of any innocent unfamiliar person. In the not too distant past, inaccurate rumours about how sexually transmitted diseases could be caught were rife, leading to countless numbers of people developing a terror of public loos.

Latrinophobia
Fear of Lavatories

Netty's mother was paranoid about public lavatories and made a tremendous fuss on car journeys, constantly schooling her children that under no circumstances were they to touch anything in a public loo. As the family trooped into the motorway services Netty's mother did not let up for a second about the dangers lurking within lavatory bowls, the plethora of germs multiplying on the flushing mechanism. Even the lavatory door handle was a harbinger of disease.

The female children became practised in loo-hovering techniques along with adopting an elaborate hand washing etiquette. Armed with a roll of kitchen towel, Netty's mother would solemnly dole out several sheets to each child and they would then use this as a protective barrier to turn off the tap, having washed their hands.

Having completed their ablutions, the entire female contingent of the family would lie in wait for an unsuspecting member of the public to enter the ladies' loos. At this point they would dart forward en masse and evacuate the loos without having to make physical contact with the door handle.

As Netty got older her disgust of public lavatories became increasingly pronounced to the extent that she did not feel that she could go to university unless the family could afford to provide her with accommodation which included an en suite bathroom.

5. Excessive stress

The source of stress can be ill-health, poor sleep, unemployment, overwork, impending exams and a host of other reasons. Equally, excessive stress can be the result of what most of us perceive as positive factors such as getting married, being made captain of a team or moving to a more desirable area. This category is of particular interest since it accounts for why people can suddenly develop a fear of something that they previously took in their stride, or even enjoyed.

I often hear from my clients that their fear came totally out of the blue and they are thoroughly mystified by the fact that they can no longer participate in activities they previously did effortlessly and even enjoyed. They are unable to pinpoint any negative experience that may have triggered their fear. Nor, as far as they are concerned, have they been suffering from stress since everything in their life seemed to be going well. An good example of this phenomenon at work was the case of Jaquetta.

Kymophobia
Fear of Sailing

Jaquetta had inherited a considerable sum of money and as a consequence was able to give up her job, which she had not enjoyed. As a result of the financial windfall, Jaquetta and her husband, Papandrou, had been able to afford a new car and a small holiday property on the Norfolk Broads. They had also booked a six-week cruise to the Caribbean, since this had always been their preferred way to spend their vacations. Several weeks before they were due to set sail, Jaquetta started to become uncomfortable about the forthcoming trip. As the anxiety symptoms escalated Jaquetta had to acknowledge the fact that she was terrified at the prospect of sailing, a pursuit which she had previously adored.

By inheriting the money, Jaquetta's lifestyle changed considerably within a short space of time. Even though this change was for the better it still involved a tremendous psychological strain. This is because most of what we do each day becomes routine and we conduct much of our life on an auto-pilot basis which conserves energy. When we experience changes in our life the brain has to apply intense focus and attention until it masters the new routine and it becomes part of our behavioural DNA. This is similar to learning any new skill, like swimming or driving a car; although initially demanding, once we have achieved competency in these skills we can do them with minimal effort. It is an ironic reality that the added stress caused by positive change in our life can cause a phobia in an arena in which we were previously not just comfortable, but which we positively enjoyed. This phenomenon is something I have met often in frequent flyers, who have previously enjoyed flying and then suddenly become aviophobic. It is particularly bewildering to the sufferer as to why they should develop a fear of something they previously did effortlessly, and needless to say this compounded Jaquetta's distress.

I will look at this category of stress, caused by what is perceived as positive change, in greater detail when I discuss how the brain works in chapter 7. For the moment it is sufficient to say that an excess of stress makes us vulnerable to developing phobias or other types of mental health problems even though there may appear to be no apparent connection.

Sometimes we can trace a phobia to an event which has happened to us, such as developing a fear of birds after having a flock of pigeons fly past us at very close range. Or we can trace a phobia to being excessively upset by something and this then being translated to the events that surrounded us at the time. An example of this could be receiving a call on your mobile while on a train journey, giving news about a friend's death. The ensuing trauma could lead to a phobia of trains.

There are times, however, where the advent of a phobia can feel totally random and the type of phobia that suddenly emerges can be extremely baffling for the individual. The following list of unusual phobias illustrates the sheer breadth of possible phobias that can mar an individual's life.

A dozen unusual phobias

Selenophobia	Fear of the moon
Pogonophobia	Fear of beards
Consecotaleophobia	Fear of chopsticks
Euphobia	Fear of hearing good news
Genuphobia	Fear of knees
Barophobia	Fear of gravity
Cacophobia	Fear of ugliness
Porphyrophobia	Fear of the colour purple
Novercaphobia	Fear of stepmothers
Plutophobia	Fear of wealth
Eurotophobia	Fear of female genitalia
Pteronophobia	Fear of being tickled

6. Phobias – Risk Factors

Factors that make us more susceptible to developing a phobia

1. Gender

Twice as many women as men develop phobias. There is a great deal of speculation as to why this is the case. The debate rages over questions such as whether women internalize their problems more than men, look after everyone else's needs and neglect their own, face greater stresses, have poorer life chances and lower self-esteem compared to men, to name but a few of the variables under discussion.

Although there is no consensus as to the degree to which these factors impact on women's mental well-being, there is general agreement that women tend to be more open about their mental health problems and seek help by visiting their doctor, which is then reflected in the statistics.

Before the reader runs away with the idea that men are much more stoical when it comes to illness, this is not entirely true, as their openness about 'man-flu' amply demonstrates! In the past, when men were the traditional bread winners, some of the reluctance to come forward and seek help was due to the fear of being discriminated against in terms of job prospects by being perceived as mentally flaky, such was the ignorance that surrounded mental health.

We have moved on a great deal since then but unfortunately this legacy still prevails to a certain extent.

2. Temperament

People with a low stress tolerance capacity will be more susceptible to developing a phobia since they are more easily alarmed and scared. Clearly a child with a shy, nervous disposition will be a more likely candidate for developing a social phobia than a confident, outgoing, extroverted sort of child.

Sadly, children of a more introverted nature can frequently become targets for bullying, since a more outgoing assertive child will be more likely to retaliate and refuse to become a victim. People who are prone to worrying and are highly sensitive may well have a hypersensitive amygdala, the 'fear centre' part of the brain furniture that I will discuss at length later on.

Benjamin Franklin once said:

'They who can give up essential liberty to obtain a little temporary safety deserve neither liberty nor safety.'

On the one hand I endorse Franklin's sentiments, which advocate a refusal to be intimidated by fear, however, I believe that a high degree of compassion and understanding must be offered to people who fall within this low stress tolerance category. This is not to say that they cannot overcome fears and phobias but one should acknowledge their tremendous courage and bravery in doing so.

3. Genetics

There is a mounting body of research which points to the fact that phobias have a genetic component. Twin studies demonstrate that identical twins have a much higher propensity towards developing the same phobia than other family members or the population at large. This is despite the twins being raised in totally separate environments, thus ruling out the nurture factor.

4. Culture

Certain phobias are more prevalent in certain cultures and some only exist at all in specific cultures. For example, Japanese culture is collectivist and places a great deal of emphasis on the importance of individuals meeting the expectations of the group. For this reason Japanese people can suffer great embarrassment and humiliation if they do not conform to social mores and rituals, since they appreciate that they will be causing considerable offence to others. This phobia is known as 'Taijin Kyofusho', and is specific to Japanese culture, and has in some extreme cases led to young Japanese students taking their own lives rather than living with their perceived disgrace and shame for not achieving top marks in their exams.

Another example of the greater proliferation of a phobia due to cultural influences is that of African Americans having a higher propensity towards developing agoraphobia. Social phobias are more common in parts of Russia compared to other demographics, which again illustrates a cultural component at work.

5. Nurture or family environment
Unsurprisingly, family dynamics play a considerable role in the likelihood of a phobia developing since a phobia is, apart from those phobias which are hard-wired (see page 11), a learned behaviour. Those in close proximity to us, like family members, have the greatest advantage in influencing our behaviour. An outgoing, confident family atmosphere will make one less susceptible to the development of a phobia, whereas being exposed to insecure, anxious family role models will increase the likelihood.

If there is a history of mental health problems within a family this will further fuel the chances of developing a phobia since a biological component may be in action too. It goes without saying that a family where abuse takes place will further increase the chances of an individual developing a phobia or indeed any other form of mental health problem.

6. Life history
From birth, your life experience will have an influence on your likelihood of developing a phobia. If you have suffered some very difficult experiences, particularly if these happened before you could talk, then they will possibly remain

unexpressed but may form the foundation for you being particularly sensitive to certain situations.

When working with clients after the 9/11 tragedy, a number of them had become phobic about loud noises, such as cars backfiring. Many of them also developed a phobia about any unexpected movements overhead. The flight of a bird or a window opening above them as they walked down the street would cause their startle response to fire off, leading to a racing heart and flinching. It is easy to see that if someone has experienced a number of traumatic events throughout their life they will be more prone to developing a phobia.

7. Age

Age plays a big part in the likelihood of developing a phobia. Specific phobias are more prevalent in young children. As mentioned previously, this is largely down to the fact that they have little experience with which to compare a frightening event and therefore will be more prone to see things in black and white terms and extrapolate a freak event to a general phenomenon.

If an adult meets an aggressive dog it is far easier to put that behaviour into context if previous encounters with the canine population had been pleasant experiences. For a small child with little comparable experience, coupled with the fact that, by virtue of their age, they are smaller and less powerful, the same event will naturally lead to a heightened evaluation of the danger of the situation.

Social phobias tend to emerge during the teen years when self-consciousness peaks. Agoraphobia is more typical in the early twenties to mid-thirties age bracket. However, all types of phobias can become manifest at any age.

8. Social factors

Evidence has emerged from various studies that current generations are generally more anxious than previous generations. This has been ascribed to there being fewer social connections as a result of the demise of the active extended family. With an increase in the impact of virtual connections via the media, such as reality TV, social networking and the like, young people more readily compare themselves to their peers.

Frequently they cannot compete with the airbrushed celebrities and find themselves wanting. Sadly, this engenders insecurity and self-loathing in youngsters, which makes them less resilient to life in general and therefore a more likely target for a phobia.

List of debilitating phobias

Some phobias impact on the sufferer on a daily basis and hence are extremely debilitating. If you recall, as mentioned previously, people with a phobia try to avoid the fear stimulus at all costs. You can readily see how the phobias listed below must cause the sufferers immense difficulties.

Anemophobia	Fear of air (drafts, wind, gusts)
Urophobia	Fear of urination
Phobophobia	Fear of light
Nyctophobia	Fear of the dark
Domophobia	Fear of houses
Decidophobia	Fear of decisions
Stasibasiphobia	Fear of standing
Chronophobia	Fear of time
Clinophobia	Fear of going to bed
Phagophobia	Fear of swallowing
Lalophobia	Fear of speaking
Anthrophobia	Fear of people

There are other phobias, which although not quite so debilitating, have the capacity to make life that little bit less fun. These are things like **oenophobia**, **gynophobia** and **decantophobia**, which are the fears of wine, women and song!

Ailurophobia
Fear of Cats

Women and cats will do as they please and men and dogs should relax and get used to the idea.
Robert A. Heinlein

In my research I have been somewhat amused to find that there are a number of powerful leaders who have endured a most discomforting relationship with cats. This gives credence to the expression that when people do not oblige and bend to our will it is 'like trying to herd cats'.

Julius Caesar, Dwight Eisenhower, Benito Mussolini and Genghis Khan were all Ailurophobic. Cats, as we know, enjoy a reputation for fierce independence, which is totally contrary to dogs. Although the canine population is adored by many of us for their magnificent qualities of loyalty, obedience and companionship there is still a sizeable number of people who are Cynophobic, which is understandable if they have been on the receiving end of a good bite!

In the next chapter we will look at what happens in the brain when we experience the powerful emotion of fear.

7. The Brain and Fear

Fear and its consequences

As mentioned earlier, fear plays a key part in a phobia. I will now explain what is happening in your brain when you register fear.

As you are aware, the brain is the most complex organ in the body and is made up of many different parts. For our purpose the relevant players in this amazing organ are the **amygdala**, or amygdalae to be more accurate, since we have been endowed with a pair of them, the **hypothalamus** and the **pituitary gland**. Away from the brain, the **adrenal glands**, which are located above each kidney, also play a significant role.

The amygdalae and the limbic system

The amygdalae are the gatekeepers, charged with the task of keeping you safe. So imagine that you have a brace of burly bouncers tucked inside your head, whose key role is to see off any threat to your continued survival. They are located in the part of the brain that is known as the **limbic system**, the place where all the emotional stuff goes on.

Pattern matching

These characters are extremely useful but not overly smart. They operate in a very rough and ready way using a process known as **pattern matching**.

This simply means that they scan all incoming sensory data for any sign of threat, and if it matches some previously stored memory, which has been deemed as harmful, you then get a reaction not dissimilar to the commotion of a fruit machine when all the apples or pears line up.

Stress hormones

But unlike a fruit machine, instead of chucking out a set of money when a match is scored, your body pumps out a cocktail of stress hormones, which will prove to be far more useful if you are attempting to fight for your life with a bad-tempered grizzly bear than trying to buy him off with cash.

The amygdalae's default position errs on the side of caution

The amygdalae's default setting is to interpret any ambiguous message as dangerous. It is far better to overreact to something that proves to be innocuous than to overlook something that proves to be lethal. The fact that we are around today is as a direct result of our ancestors having this facility, which kept them alive to parent the next generation.

Life without our amygdalae

As an aside, some interesting research has been conducted into how an organism would react if it did not have interventions from the amygdalae. Rats who had their amygdalae removed showed absolutely no fear in the presence of cats.

Similarly, humans who had lost amygdalae functionality as a result of a stroke were incapable of decoding the emotion of fear from facial expressions. This means that while people might be running away in terror as a result of having seen an approaching tsunami, those without amygdalae functionality would look on blandly, incapable of reading the imminent threat. As you can well appreciate, the consequences could well be fatal.

The chain of command

So returning to our former theme, all stimuli received from any of your five senses – sight, sound, touch, taste or smell – are filtered for threat. Any incoming information that remotely matches a stored memory in the 'danger' file will cause a knock-on reaction.

This chain reaction consists of the amygdalae communicating with a part of the brain called the hypothalamus, which then causes the adrenal-cortical system and the sympathetic nervous system to be activated. The activation of the adrenal-cortical system results in the pituitary gland secreting a hormone known as ACTH (adrenocorticotropic), which causes the adrenal cortex to release a vast cocktail of 30 hormones into the bloodstream. These hormones then prime the body to either fight or run away from the threat. The sympathetic nervous system collaborates with this enterprise by bringing the body to an intense state of alertness by priming the major muscles to be ready for flight or combat. At the same time, the sympathetic nervous system also acts on the adrenal medulla causing the release of further hormones, noradrenalin and adrenalin into the bloodstream. The combination of all this neural and hormonal activity is what culminates in the fight or flight response – an instantaneous reaction that takes place throughout your body with the sole intention of ensuring your survival.

The cortex

Now it would be remiss of me to not mention another key character in this drama and that is the **cortex**, which operates in a very different fashion to the amygdalae. The cortex is the thinking part of the brain and is a relatively new piece of kit in terms of our evolutionary development. It is responsible for what makes us human. In this part of the brain we weigh up situations, compare options and make choices and decisions. It carries out the executive function of the brain and is sensible, rational and wise.

Sensory data has two routes

Data from the five senses has routes to both the cortex and the amygdalae, and if it is non-threatening information the amygdalae leave it to the cortex to deal with whatever needs to be remembered, decided upon or actioned, and they take a little siesta.

However, if the amygdalae score a pattern match from the incoming data, when compared with the stored memories in the danger file, then all hell breaks loose.

A metaphorical portcullis in the brain slams shut, denying any access or action from the thinking part of the brain; the cortex is temporarily put out of business. I am sure that many readers who suffer from a phobia will recognize that this is the stage where you look on helplessly while your body is launched into a full-scale panic attack, despite your best efforts to try to get a grip of the situation.

Amygdalae in command

You are now in the hands of the amygdalae. In fairness to them, when you need to get yourself out of a hole these are the best guys to give you instant directions and critical information to get you to where you need to go to avoid being gobbled up by a Yeti. You don't even have to think since your guardian angel bouncers have all the data at their fingertips and can call upon crucial stored information that you didn't even know existed. You are now under unconscious control.

Instant reaction

Think about your reactions when something has unexpectedly been knocked over and you seemingly miraculously catch it before it hits the floor. It is your amygdalae friends that you need to thank, since they were on to the job long before your cortex had even registered what was happening to your best china vase, let alone thought what to do about it.

Emergency survival mode

What is happening to you in biological terms is that you have switched course from **conscious** long-term survival mode (cortex in charge) to **unconscious** short-term emergency survival mode (amygdalae in charge), so you have little control over the two guys at the helm.

Now this is an excellent arrangement if there is a genuine threat, since your cortex would be of little use to you in a situation where an instant reaction is required. Remember the cortex is the cool-headed character who will methodically consult stored records in a calm and measured manner and then thoughtfully deliberate on what plan of action would appear to be best to select.

In moments of real danger, the rapidity of the reaction could literally make the difference between life and death, which is why the alarm fired off by the amygdalae is so crucial to our survival.

Emergency mode designed for physical threat only

Now here's the rub. As you can appreciate, this wonderful survival mechanism dates way back in our history and originally evolved to enable us to combat **physical threat**. Today, thankfully, physical threat is a relatively rare occurrence and the chance of being consumed by predators is singularly remote. We are still, alas, vulnerable to accidents, muggings and other unfortunate circumstances, but by and large, unless one is living in a war zone, we have little regular need to fire off our fight or flight response.

Inappropriate use of survival mechanism

Yet despite the relative degree of safety, many of us employ this survival response inappropriately to combat psychological threats, which was never the purpose of its original design. A mechanism whose function is to increase our strength to fight the threat or boost our speed to run away from danger is totally useless when it comes to panicking about the state of our marriage, the health of our child or the paucity of our future pension pot.

In fact it is positively injurious, since being prone to frequent panic attacks can sometimes damage relationships or compromise our ability to hold down a job to provide for our future.

A prehistoric tool in a modern world

Our ancestors led fairly unsophisticated lives in comparison to ours and most of their daily problems consisted of hunting and trying to stay safe from marauding tribes and predators. The survival mechanism was perfect for these purposes and enabled man to thrive in a physically hostile environment. Evolution is a very slow process and it will be many millennia before we adapt biologically to our current way of living, which is physically fairly safe but psychologically very threatening indeed.

8. Anxiety and Panic Attacks

Below you will find the cast of characters who perform in the **Anticipatory Anxiety and Panic Attack Drama**. Bang on cue they kick into action when you and your phobia meet up, or even anticipate meeting up.

The Anxiety and Panic Attack Drama
Starring

The Cast	The Role
The Amygdalae	Guardians of emotional memories and deployers of the fight or flight response, by alerting the hypothalamus.
The Hypothalamus	Releaser of hormones, which control the pituitary gland.
The Pituitary Gland	Master gland and director of the endocrine glands including the adrenal glands.
Adrenal Glands	Pair of glands which secrete stress hormones, such as adrenaline and noradrenaline.
Cortex	Usually the guy in charge but not this time – his role has changed to 'unwilling bystander and witness to the panic experience' – a somewhat passive part due to the amygdalae being in control and short-term emergency survival protocol being in operation.

You have now met the key characters, who jointly bring about this heightened state of alert, which is known as a state of anxiety, or if the symptoms become exaggerated, a **panic attack**. We will soon look closely at the transformations that happen to your emotions, thoughts, body and behaviour when this happens. But before we do so, it might be helpful to read some of the comments below that my clients have made, describing this powerful experience. I am sure that some of these statements will have a resonance with your own experience if you have suffered from a phobia.

'It's terrifying. I totally lose control over my body; it just seems to do its own thing.'

'It's like an unstoppable tsunami, I feel totally engulfed in a tide of fear.'

'My heart races so fast and bangs so hard, I feel that my chest will explode.'

'My mind seems to go blank and all I want to do is escape.'

'I try to concentrate but it's impossible.'

'It is the most desperate feeling in the world and I just want to be put out of my misery.'

'I can feel the panic welling up in me as my legs and hands tremble, and I'm covered in sweat.'

'At first everything feels surreal and initially I look around in embarrassment hoping that nobody has noticed that I've started to cry. As the panic gets worse I know what's coming and I no longer care who is watching me, I just want to run away.'

'I get pins and needles and find it hard to swallow.'

'The more I hyperventilate, the more I feel that I can't breathe.'

'My heart pounds so hard that I'm convinced I'm about to have a heart attack.'

'A panic attack is the worst experience I have ever endured in my life.'

Intense anxiety/panic attacks are all-consuming

As the above comments amply demonstrate, an intense state of anxiety, or even worse a panic attack, is not something one can forget in a hurry.

Panic attacks are all-encompassing, and by this I mean that their impact on you is at a physical, psychological, behavioural and emotional level. The reason why it is all-consuming is that all stops are pulled out to warn you that you are in grave danger and need to run away or deal with the situation immediately.

It would not be much of a survival mechanism if you could choose to ignore it, so the message to **ESCAPE OR FIGHT** is delivered with both barrels. Now we will look at the mechanics of how that powerful message is delivered by exploring the role of **anxiety**.

KEY TERM

What is anxiety?

A phobia comes under the umbrella of anxiety disorders and therefore it is important to appreciate the difference between fear and anxiety since both play a vital part in phobia acquisition and maintenance. Fear, as you now know, is the powerful negative emotion which we experience when we believe ourselves to be in imminent danger.

Fear is the feeling we encounter when actually faced with the threat. It is immediate and in the here and now.

Anxiety on the other hand is a form of preparation for the future threat by means of worrying. It is worth noting that we also use the terms nervous, apprehensive or anxious interchangeably.

Anxiety is the state of being worried, demonstrated by hyper vigilance, uncertainty and tension. It is the brain's way of rehearsing for a future threat.

The example below demonstrates the subtle difference between these two concepts, fear and anxiety.

THINK ABOUT IT

Vermiphobia
Fear of Worms

If I am phobic about worms and one crawls across the flagstone in front of me I will experience FEAR. However, if I have been asked by the Parent–Teacher Association to help with the planting of a new commemorative garden next weekend then I will experience ANXIETY. The difference being that anxiety is directed towards a future threat.

Fear and anxiety are not villains

Useful anxiety

It is only fair to say that anxiety, like fear, is a normal and natural phenomenon, which we all experience from time to time. It is also beneficial, providing it doesn't get out of control or become a regular feature in our life against an unreal threat such as a phobia.

Appropriate anxiety is what motivates us to renew our car insurance when it expires, because we worry about the consequences of being involved in an accident without cover. Appropriate anxiety is responsible for pushing us to confirm meetings with colleagues rather than risk a wasted journey if we are worried that they may have forgotten our arrangement.

Adrenalin – the extra edge to help you perform

Any actor will tell you that unless they feel a little nervous before going on stage then they will not deliver their best performance, since they will have stopped worrying or caring about how the audience will react.

Appropriate anxiety is what gives us a little nudge to prepare thoroughly, since a moderate amount of adrenalin will both motivate us and help us to focus our attention on the task in hand. Athletes and performers use that adrenalin rush judiciously to ensure that they give of their best.

Some people even describe themselves as adrenalin junkies and participate in extreme sports because they like the sensation of being geed up by just the right amount of adrenalin to enable them to stretch themselves further. It is an exhilarating experience to get closer to our potential and this buzz can become highly addictive. I have some close relatives who fit into this category and they are constantly seeking the next adventure to enjoy the excitement and thrill of the adrenaline rush.

Dissipation of stress hormones

The main concept to grasp in the above examples is that the anxiety has caused stress hormones to be released into the bloodstream, in turn causing the body to become aroused. The hormones have then been put to use – that is, some action has been taken which causes them to dissipate – and the body then returns to its pre-aroused state: job done. The athlete has run his race, the actor has delivered his performance, and you have contacted your insurers and renewed your policy and so forth.

Useless anxiety

What people with a phobia need to worry about is useless anxiety. This is anxiety that is simply non-productive and does not serve a useful purpose. As explained above, the whole point of bringing your body into an aroused state is to enable it to complete an action. If we worry and deluge ourselves with stress hormones and do nothing with them, we simply put ourselves through extreme discomfort for nothing. So to lie awake in bed worrying about whether we are going to get up in time for work in the morning is useless if we don't take the action of setting our alarm clock. To spend time fretting over whether we will pass our exams is pointless if it doesn't compel us to pick up our studies and revise.

Worse-than-useless anxiety

Because a phobia is based on a fake threat in the first place, any arousal caused by anxiety can only be dissipated by avoidance (flight), which sadly only makes the phobia stronger. We could try to use the other option and attack (fight) the button, the elevator, the thunder, the bridge and so on, but I think that you would agree that this too would be a fairly useless response.

My wellington boot: A cautionary tale about not taking appropriate action

I like to take my Labrador, Faustus, for an early morning walk in the woods. I have on several occasions damaged my wellington boots on a sharp stone or branch, causing a hairline scratch across the boot. I am usually only made aware of the problem when I sense that my foot has become slightly damp. Obviously the sensible thing to do would be to repair it as soon as

I get home. I know that I should do this immediately and have the all-too-familiar saying, *'a stitch in time saves nine'* ringing in my ears.

However, I never really got round to dealing with the problem. I always reckoned that I was far too busy and I found myself the next morning, and each following morning for the next few weeks, putting on the slightly damp boot, while looking out anxiously for any sign of rain. This was despite the constant nagging of the voice of anxiety saying, **'you really must do something about this'**.

Now the boot, just like a phobia, was not going to get better on its own. In fact it got progressively worse and very soon reached a point when it became the total focus of my daily walk. I stopped noticing the flowers and trees and found myself totally absorbed with the task of selecting which path to take in accordance with the number of puddles I would encounter. On account of my dodgy boot I was orchestrating the walk to **AVOID** getting my foot soaked, causing us to miss out on the more scenic routes much to my displeasure and Faustus' irritation. The long and the short of it was that **my boot was calling the shots and dictating the route of our walk**.

Does this sound familiar with regard to your phobia? This was certainly a case of the tail wagging the dog. On top of the walk no longer being pleasant and the nagging anxiety I was enduring, I had also caused myself the extra burden of having to wash endless socks and boot-liners as a result of my injudicious behaviour.

It was not until I returned home one morning, utterly cold and miserable, with a totally squelching boot, that I decided enough was enough and got around to purchasing a new pair of boots. Why did I let this simple situation get out of hand, you might ask? My excuse would have been that I was too busy and didn't have time to repair the boots or go shopping for a new pair.

The reality is that I did eventually manage to find the time but had compromised the quality of my morning walk and wasted considerably more time in the long run by not **taking action** immediately to deal with my problem. I had learnt to my cost that:

Procrastination is the thief of time.
Charles Dickens

Are you allowing your life to be screwed up by not taking the necessary steps to deal with your phobia? Stop tiptoeing around the gremlin and deal with him NOW. By not doing so you are effectively capping your potential.

Ask yourself the following questions:

1. Are you living with nagging anxiety as a result of your phobia?

2. Are you contorting your life to avoid situations that will trigger your phobia?

3. Is the quality of your life being compromised by your phobia?

4. Are you wasting time, money, opportunities and happiness in living with your phobia?

5. Are you wasting energy in trying to hide your phobia from others by constantly having to make up excuses?

If you have answered yes to any of these questions then you owe it to yourself to **take action** and do something about it **NOW**.

> *Never put off for tomorrow what you can do today.*
> Thomas Jefferson

 Life is short enough; so don't waste it by compromising your happiness.

I was once given an embroidered cushion as a gift from a girlfriend. The inscription on the cushion reads:

'Life's too short, so let's have pudding first.'

We would be wise to heed the advice and make sure that we enjoy each day of our lives, and that certainly must mean not being held to ransom by a phobia.

Anticipatory anxiety

I have chosen as an example Aviophobia, the fear of flying, as this is an area in which I have worked with numerous clients. Many of them claim that the anticipatory anxiety starts from the minute they open the holiday brochures. This can be months before the planned vacation, and it totally destroys their quality of life during the build-up to the holiday. I frequently hear refrains similar to the one below from one of my clients:

> 'I know I should be looking forward to going abroad to such an amazing destination, but all I can focus on is how am I going to get through the flight there and back.'

What starts off as slight anxiety months ahead of the trip gradually builds to an unbearable pitch and might well culminate in the sufferer calling off the entire holiday the day or week before the departure date. To live for weeks or months with a steady cocktail of stress hormones dripping into the bloodstream is incredibly wearing and upsetting to say the least.

Impact of worrying on sleep patterns

Ongoing anxiety, as well as blighting the time that you are awake and worrying, also takes its toll on the quality of your sleep at night. This is because the body has been primed to a state of alertness throughout the day without anything happening to dissipate this position (that is, there has been no fight or flight).

In order to keep the integrity of this mechanism so that it will work the following day (a bit like a battery needing to be recharged) the brain will ensure that the sufferer spends longer in the REM (Rapid Eye Movement) phase of sleep. This dream state enables the worrier to discharge the built-up stress in a metaphorical way by using a dream sequence to achieve catharsis or emotional release.

Sleep that knits up the raveled sleeve of care.
The death of each day's life, sore labour.
Shakespeare

This is not a problem in itself; however, by spending an inordinate amount of time in the REM state the body is denied its full quota of time in the Slow Wave Recuperative sleep mode, which ensures that the body is well rested and the immune system boosted.

Put quite simply, today's worry becomes tonight's poor sleep due to a bigger dose of REM sleep, which will result in a deficiency of slow wave sleep and thus you will wake up tired despite the fact that you might well have slept for many hours.

I hope that this chapter has alerted you to the cost of unproductive worrying, both while you are awake and while you are asleep. In the next chapter we will look more closely at the symptoms generated by this worry, which as you will see are not inconsiderable. Keep in mind that the worry experienced by someone with a phobia is always unproductive worrying, since the fear is irrational in the first place.

9. Symptoms of Anxiety/Panic Attack

The four domains

As I have already intimated, the symptoms caused by worrying are extensive and will impact on an individual in a multitude of ways. There will be **emotional**, **behavioural**, **cognitive** and **physiological** changes as a result of the anxiety. These changes are known as symptoms, and below you will see a selection of them under the four domains mentioned above.

Emotional symptoms:

Anger
Tension
Insecurity
Guilt
Depression
Sadness
Exhaustion
Irritability
Feelings of uselessness
Jitters
Impatience
Fear
Edginess

Uneasiness
Helplessness
Feeling like a victim
Hopelessness

Behavioural symptoms:
Avoidance
Lack of focus
Insomnia
Sleeping pattern changes
Clenching jaw
Twitching
Forgetfulness
Yawning
Grinding teeth
Hyperventilation
Startling easily
Cravings
Impaired coordination
Running away
Jolting awake
Withdrawal from people and activities
Unsteadiness
Speech problems
Fidgeting
Changes in appetite

Psychological/mind symptoms:
Fear of being rejected
Sense of impending doom
Worrying about what people think of you
Loss of confidence
Fear of losing control
Being easily distracted
Fear of dying
Preoccupation with health concerns
Short-term memory loss
Confusion
Low self-esteem
High insecurity
Inability to control thinking
Surreal experience
Feelings of déjà vu
A sense of oddness

Physiological/bodily symptoms:
Pins and needles
Numbness
Indigestion
Bloating
Sensitive eyes
Tense muscles
Heart palpitations
Headaches
Diarrhoea

Vomiting
Burning sensations on the skin
Shaking/trembling
Abdominal pain
Frequent urination
Aches and pains
Weak muscles
Tight muscles
Nausea
Hot and cold spells
Shortness of breath

When does anxiety turn into a panic attack?

In some people the above symptoms build up and reach a crescendo, which is known as a **panic attack**. This is a perfectly normal phenomenon resulting from the intensification of the symptoms, but is nevertheless a terrifying and overwhelming ordeal for the individual.

People, when experiencing a panic attack, frequently feel that they are losing their mind, about to pass out or have a heart attack, or are about to die, to mention but a few of the terrors I have been told about from my clients.

Meet the predator

What is actually happening at this point is that short-term emergency survival mode has been put into action. So the body shifts priorities to enable it to be as fast and powerful as possible to defeat or evade the threat. The pupils will dilate to let in more information, sweating will occur to cool the body down since the extra heat generated by muscular activity will cause an increase in body temperature.

Non-essential processes like digestion shut down as blood vessels in the gut constrict to enable blood to be pumped at a powerful rate to the major muscles in the legs and arms for running away from or fighting the danger. This explains the gastrointestinal symptoms some people experience during panic attacks, as well as the urge to urinate, as all will naturally make you lighter and able to flee more quickly from the danger! Seems unpleasant, but if you were legging it from a hungry lion you might be grateful.

You would also be eternally grateful for the giant shot of adrenalin that your adrenal glands generously delivered at the sight of the lion's jaws, as they were about to close over your head. It is the stress hormones that have given you that 'va va voom' quality which has enabled you to hightail it to safety.

Fear response is an inexact science

The problem is that this response is a tad over the top if instead of a lion your feared object is an ant or a gerbil! Sadly, the amygdalae, as I have already explained, are a rather rough and ready pair and they only know how to offer you the same deal. It's a sort of one-size-fits-all package.

How long do panic attacks last?

A panic attack may last up to twenty minutes maximum and frequently passes after five to ten minutes. However, some people become so distressed by their symptoms, that they may experience multiple panic attacks by convincing themselves that they are about to die, thus further fuelling the panic and hence the duration of the attack. In these circumstances it may feel to the sufferer that they are enduring one seamless lengthy panic attack, rather than a series of panic attacks or just extremely high anxiety levels.

It is entirely understandable that these overwhelming sensations cause tremendous fear in the individual, but acceptance of what is happening to them is the fastest way to make the attack stop.

I often recommend the **ALERT** technique to my clients to help prevent the vicious cycle of multiple panic attacks happening to them. By having a technique that helps you to monitor what is happening, you will be less prone to exaggerating the symptoms or their duration.

A – Accept what you are feeling and what is happening to you without getting angry or upset by your emotion of fear and the physical symptoms with which it is accompanied.

A panic attack is exceptionally unpleasant but don't fight it, just go with it. Be like a surfer who rides the waves rather than struggling and battling against them, since your emotions are more powerful than your thoughts. Recognize that you have experienced these attacks before and have always come through them and they do not harm you. Accept the tide of your emotions and go with the flow.

L – Look at what is happening to you and note the changes. For example, your heart might be racing, you may be perspiring profusely and your legs might be shaking. Use this information to give yourself a score between one and ten (one being totally calm and ten feeling demented). This task forces you to observe yourself, and you should see that the score will fluctuate and eventually come down, since a panic attack is a **SHORT**-TERM emergency measure and can **NOT** continue indefinitely.

E – Enact normal behaviour. This means stay in the situation rather than running away. Avoidance is tempting as it will give you short-term relief but it will also strengthen your phobia. Also, as soon as you are able, try to reintroduce normal breathing patterns and allow your muscles to relax.

R – Repeat the steps above until the panic passes. You will recognize this point approaching as your score between one and ten decreases.

T – Think positively. Remember that it is negative thinking which caused the panic in the first place, so do not re-indoctrinate yourself with further negative thoughts.

By keeping the above in mind you will come out the other side of the panic attack far more smoothly and faster. Just like the surfer who rides the wave and is swiftly delivered on to the shore.

Now that you have an understanding of the nature of phobias and what is happening to you, we can now move on to exploring in the next section how they can be overcome. I very much hope that you are keen and determined to set yourself free of their power over your life.

The key to life is accepting challenges.
Once someone stops doing this, he's dead.
Bette Davis

SECTION B:
Overcoming Phobias

10. How to Get Help and the Types of Treatment Available

An ounce of action is worth a ton of theory.
Ralph Waldo Emerson

In this chapter I would like to give you a clear idea about what will happen when you seek help, particularly professional help, for overcoming your phobia. Many people are unsure about what to expect when they visit their GP and have questions about whether they will be treated by the GP or referred to a specialist.

When they are referred, they may have concerns about what the actual treatment entails, and wonder if they will be offered medication, psychological therapies or a combination of the two. I will briefly mention a number of talking therapies, but will discuss in depth two of the main approaches for treating phobias in later chapters. I will also give an indication of some of the types of medication that may be offered to people suffering from a phobia.

Steps to defeat a phobia
Step 1 – Admit you need help
Step 2 – Choose appropriate help
Step 3 – Carry out the selected treatment

Step 1 – Admitting you need help

The first step to be taken when tackling a phobia is to acknowledge that you have a problem in the first place. As mentioned earlier, a huge percentage of the population sit on their phobia for many years before taking the necessary steps to deal with it. Some are in total denial and claim that it is not a problem that they can't travel by some particular mode of transport or visit family members who own pets.

People orchestrate their lives around avoidance of their particular phobic trigger and claim that it is no skin off their nose to have to do so. Comments like, 'why should I want to go abroad when I haven't visited everywhere in my own country' or, 'if they want to see me then they are more than welcome to come to my home without bringing their dog', abound. These excuses help to assuage the discomfort that people experience when they are trying to deny the fact that they have a problem in the first place.

I have met several clients who only acknowledged their problem with flying when they needed to seek medical treatment abroad or were unable to take up a wonderful job prospect which required a certain amount of foreign travel. Similarly, I have worked with clients who have not addressed their fear of heights or claustrophobia until their work has relocated to a high-rise building, requiring them to use stairs or lifts.

As we will see in chapter 16, wherein we discuss the 4Rs Paradigm, the brain works on expectations and it is imperative that you give it a clear directive that you plan to change the status quo and address your fear, otherwise it will default to its autopilot position and continue with its established pattern of avoidance.

Step 2 – Choosing the appropriate help

Having admitted that something is preventing you from living your life in accordance with your choices, the next step is to get some sort of help. If you could overcome your phobia entirely on your own the chances are that this would have happened already. You may find that reading a self-help book, such as this one, or attending a self-help group is sufficient. Or you may need to enlist the support of a friend, family member or colleague to help you to address your fear.

Finally, it may be that the best course of action for you is to seek professional help. Regardless of the option you choose the key thing is to follow through your decision immediately. Remember that the gremlin will encourage you to procrastinate because that is in its best interest!

a) Self-help book or self-help group

There are many self-help books on the market that deal with anxiety and phobias and depending upon where you live there may be self-help groups in your area. A good place to discover what is on offer in your location is the Internet and in the local library.

b) Support from a friend, family member or colleague

If you decide to enlist the support of a friend, family member or colleague, be very careful about who you choose to assist you. You need the help of someone that will be compassionate and understanding about your problem but also able to help you to meet your challenges without rushing in to the situation to rescue you.

Some people lack sufficient empathy to appreciate the terror experienced by someone with a phobia and can be totally unsympathetic and cavalier, urging the sufferer to, 'just get on with it'. On the other hand there are those who cannot bear to watch pain and suffering and so can't stay strong enough to offer support.

I have worked with clients whose attempts to overcome their phobia have been actively undermined as a result of the benign intentions of their partners. Their inability to tolerate their loved one's struggle in the face of their fear has led them to remove the problem by saying such things as, 'if it makes you so anxious going for an interview then don't go, we don't really need the extra income', or, 'we won't go to the restaurant if you're so upset; I'm more than happy to eat in'. This type of behaviour, although well-intentioned, is exactly the opposite of what a person with a phobia needs.

Below is one of my favourite readings about the Emperor Moth, which brilliantly encapsulates this concept.

The story of the Emperor Moth

The need to be stretched – facing struggles in life makes us strong

A man found a cocoon of the Emperor Moth and took it home to watch it emerge. One day a small opening appeared and for several hours the moth struggled but couldn't seem to force its body past a certain point.

Deciding that something was wrong, the man took scissors and snipped the remaining bit of cocoon. The moth emerged easily, its body large and swollen, the wings small and shrivelled.

He expected that in a few hours the wings would spread out in their natural beauty, but they did not. Instead of developing into a creature free to fly, the moth spent its life dragging around a swollen body and shrivelled wings.

The constricting cocoon and the struggle necessary to pass through the tiny opening are Nature's way of forcing fluid from the body into the wings. The 'merciful' snip was, in reality, cruel. Sometimes the struggle is exactly what we need.

c) Professional help

There are a number of professionals who work with people suffering from phobias and it is useful to have an understanding of their various roles and what you can expect if referred to one of them. Some of them will use talking therapies alone, or combine such treatment with medication.

There are many different types of drugs prescribed for the treatment of anxiety-based disorders, and later in this chapter we will look at some of them. First of all let us take a brief look at some of the practitioners you may encounter if you seek professional help. The institutions listed here are UK-based, but there are equivalents all over the world.

i) General Practitioner (GP)

Your GP is the most obvious person to call upon when seeking help with a phobia. A GP will have undergone medical training and will have a licence to legally practise medicine in this country, whether privately or through the NHS. The General Medical Council (GMC) issues this licence. GPs may treat you themselves, depending on their expertise in the area of phobias, or refer you to one of the professionals below.

ii) Psychiatrist

A psychiatrist is someone who has trained for five years as a doctor followed by a further two years' work in hospitals before being eligible to specialize in psychiatry. To successfully complete the professional exams of the Royal College of Psychiatrists takes another four years. Because of their medical training they are allowed to prescribe medication. Frequently, people suffering from psychological problems will be referred to a psychiatrist who will prescribe medication and oversee the treatment while referring the patient to a psychotherapist or counsellor for a course of therapy, such as Exposure Therapy.

iii) Clinical Psychologist

A clinical psychologist will have a degree in psychology, three years' work experience in a healthcare setting, followed by three years of clinical training to achieve their doctorate. Clinical psychologists are registered as practitioners with the Health Professions Council (HPC). Clinical psychologists often specialize in particular problems (e.g. bipolar disorder) and/or particular therapies (e.g. Cognitive Behavioural Therapy).

iv) Chartered Psychologist

A chartered psychologist will not usually have a medical background but will have met the necessary requirements set down by the British Psychological Society.

v) Counsellor or Psychotherapist

Training in counselling and psychotherapy can be very varied and some practitioners may have specific training in medicine and psychology, although the vast majority of practitioners do not. They use what is known as talking therapies such as Person-Centred, Psychodynamic, Systemic and Integrative Therapies. There are literally hundreds of different types of therapies available.

Main therapies for treating phobias

The main therapies used for treating phobias are: Cognitive Behavioural Therapy and Systematic Desensitization Therapy. Many practitioners also use combinations made up of, for example, Neurolinguistic Programming, Schema Therapy, Time Line Therapy and the Human Givens Fast Rewind Technique.

Be aware that the titles of 'counsellor' or 'psychotherapist' are not protected, so it is advisable to consult with practitioners who have membership of professional bodies such as the National Counselling Society (NCS) or the British Association for Counselling and Psychotherapy (BACP), or the equivalent governing body in your country.

There are many professional bodies that are associated with the therapeutic approach offered by the practitioner, such as the British Association for Behavioural and Cognitive Psychotherapies (BABCP) or the British Association for the Person Centred Approach (BAPCA).

Selecting a practitioner

(i) The therapeutic relationship is a key part of therapy so make sure that you feel comfortable with your practitioner, and if not, seek out someone else.

(ii) All bona fide practitioners in the United Kingdom have supervision, so be wary of any practitioner who cannot give you the name of their supervisor.

(iii) There are some excellent practitioners who do not have membership of professional bodies; however, unless you are following a personal recommendation, it is safer to elect to use someone with professional membership. This ensures some form of redress, should your practitioner not deliver the service offered to the expected standard.

(iv) As part of their personal development, all practitioners are expected to be non-defensive and authentic. Feel free to ask questions of your practitioner with regard to their training, qualifications and experience.

Step 3 – Carrying out selected treatment

Initial assessment

Assuming you are seeking professional help, every practitioner will vary with regard to how they conduct an initial interview with the patient/client. However, below is a range of questions you can generally expect to be asked when seeking help.

1. What is the problem?

2. Has there been a specific activating event of which you are aware (bitten by a dog, fallen down some steps, been in a car crash, etc.)?

3. How long have you been suffering from the phobia (useful to explain if it has become more prominent recently, been overcome in the past but re-emerged, etc.)?

4. How serious is your reaction to the phobic stimulus (useful to give historic examples of panic attacks, etc.)?

5. How far is this impacting on your life (e.g. threatening employment, housebound, experiencing poor sleep, obsessive thoughts, etc.)?

6. Is there anything else that is concerning you (concomitant problems like MS or depression, etc.)?

7. What else has been happening in your life over the past six months that is different (i.e. any changes, positive or negative, such as moving house, bereavement, getting a new job, etc.)?

Medication

Depending on your circumstances it may be appropriate for you to consider medication to assist in dealing with panic and anxiety. It is important that you appreciate that medication on its own will alleviate the symptoms but will not cure the 'problem'. Once the medication stops, the symptoms may well return. However, medication is sometimes offered alongside a course of therapy and is then gradually withdrawn, in accordance with your medical practitioner's instructions.

The upside of medication is that, for many, it can yield rapid and effective relief from the distressing symptoms of anxiety and panic, but the downside is that it often masks the underlying issues causing the anxiety, which can be more effectively dealt with through therapeutic intervention. When considering whether this is the best way forward for dealing with a phobia I strongly recommend that you discuss the positives and negatives of using medication with both your therapist and medical practitioner, and make an informed choice in line with your own desired outcome based on their recommendations.

The following questions will help you to decide if medication is the right choice for you:

1. What are ALL the options available to me, both on the NHS and privately?

2. If I decide to utilize the medication alongside having therapy, is it likely to be more productive than therapy on its own?

3. What types of medication are available and appropriate for me?

4. What are the possible negative side effects of the medication that you are recommending as most suitable for me?

5. How long is treatment likely to continue?

6. What is the minimum and maximum dosage and what is the best way of knowing what the correct dosage is?

7. If this treatment is ineffective, what would be the next steps?

8. If I have to take medication for other health problems, is this type of drug compatible?

9. What are the chances of my becoming addicted or dependent on the medication?

10. Will I have to restrict myself from consuming alcohol or particular foods whilst taking the medication?

11. How easy is it to withdraw from the medication?

12. If you were in my position what would you do?

Possible types of medication

There is a wide variety of medication available; below are the types that you are most likely to encounter in the treatment of phobias:

Anti-anxiety drugs – benzodiazepines

Types: Valium (diazepam), Klonopin (clonazepam), Xanax (alprazolam) and Ativan (lorazepam)

These are minor tranquilizers that slow down the central nervous system, which will help you to feel calmer. They act swiftly and can bring relief from the symptoms in as little as half an hour.

Side effects do happen occasionally and may include dizziness, nausea, double vision, depression, slow reflexes, slurred speech, memory loss, clumsiness, drowsiness or impaired thinking.

Concerns
The slowing down of reflexes is of particular concern as this can result in an increased risk of having an accident. This is particularly prevalent in the elderly. Because of the potentially addictive nature of these drugs, people who already have or have had a problem with substance abuse should be very cautious. Pregnant and breastfeeding women should likely avoid these drugs unless strongly recommended by a medical practitioner as they might impact adversely on the foetus or breastfeeding baby.

Cautions
Although this is the most widely prescribed type of medication worldwide, it has very occasionally, when taken long-term, caused suicidal thoughts and emotional flatness, since it blocks both anxiety and pleasure. These drugs should never be taken in conjunction with alcohol. Furthermore, you should check with your practitioner or pharmacist to find out if they are compatible with other

prescription or non-prescription drugs you may be taking, such as sleeping tablets and allergy medication.

In some people, benzodiazepines can lead to intense irritability and even increased anxiety. For these reasons it is imperative that you keep in touch with your practitioner so that together you can monitor the side effects and decide if it is better to discontinue and try something else.

Antidepressants

Types: Selective Serotonin Reuptake Inhibitors (SSRIs) e.g. Prozac, Seroxat, Cipramil, Welbutrin and Sertraline (brand names). Monoamine Oxidase Inhibitors (MAOIs). Tricyclic Antidepressants (TCAs)

The advantage of these drugs is that they can lead to less dependency, but the disadvantage is that they take approximately four to six weeks to take effect. They are also better recommended when anxiety is coupled with depression and may be given alongside the minor tranquillizers.

Betablockers

e.g. Atenolol (Tenormin), Propranolol (Inderal)

This type of medication works by inhibiting the effects of the stress hormones that are released in your body when you feel anxious and panicky. It does this on a physical level only, by slowing down your heart rate and decreasing the shaking and dizziness, but it does not prevent you from worrying. However, if it is the fear of the physical symptoms that exacerbates your worrying then these drugs would be helpful on a psychological level too. These are often prescribed in conjunction with the minor tranquilizers listed above.

↘ IF YOU ↙
REMEMBER
ONE
↗ THING ↖ All drugs carry risk factors, so always explore other options as well. If you and your practitioner decide to go down this route, make sure that it is for the least duration and least dosage level possible to achieve the desired results. At all times ensure that the course of treatment is closely monitored and taken as directed, and never withdraw from the medication without first discussing it with the prescriber.

Therapies

There is a vast array of available therapies for the treatment of phobias: such as Gestalt, Psychodynamic, Schema, Existential, Depth, Emotion-Focused, Rogerian and Emotional Transformation therapies, to name but a few. Many distinctive techniques are used by various practitioners, such as Hypnosis or Eye Movement Desensitization and Reprocessing (EMDR). The discussion of, or even mention of, all of these hundreds of existing therapies is not within the scope of this small book.

It is however worth pointing out the importance of checking out the various therapies before embarking upon a course of treatment. If the practitioner has no professional memberships and the proposed treatment has no available literature on the Internet from which you could form an edu-cated opinion, then extreme caution should be exercised.

So to recap the key points of this chapter: we must first acknowledge our problem; take steps to find out what help is available; and most importantly of all we should embrace and accept that help with determination and resolve.

In the next chapters I will describe two of the main approaches to treatment, known as Systematic Desensitization Therapy (a type of exposure therapy) and Cognitive Behavioural Therapy, along with my own 4Rs Paradigm.

11. Exposure Therapies

Systematic Desensitization Therapy (SDT)

Systematic Desensitization Therapy, which I will refer to as SDT, is one of the most popular and effective treatments for phobias. It is also known as a form of **exposure therapy**, of which there are several types. It was developed in the 1950s by a South African psychiatrist, Joseph Wolpe, and has been used widely in phobia treatment ever since.

This approach involves the person who has a phobia being exposed to the **phobic stimulus** (what they are afraid of) by gradual degrees. For example, if someone was phobic about snails they would first of all look at a cartoon picture of a snail and then a photograph of a snail, followed by a film showing a snail and so on – right up to the point where they actually confront a snail in the flesh.

Systematic

It is called **systematic** because it applies a fixed planned process or system. In this case the process is a methodical gradual exposure to the feared situation or object. This might be someone's fear of having to sit an exam or cross roads, which is a situational phobia, or a specific fear like a phobia of moths or paper. In all cases, the programme would involve the frightened person being exposed initially to their least anxiety-provoking encounter and end with their most frightening confrontation of the phobic stimulus. There would be many steps between these two points, which is why it is termed a **gradual exposure** form of therapy.

Desensitization

It is called **desensitization** because the therapy will slowly bring about the gradual reduction of the intensity of a person's level of sensitivity (upset) towards the phobic stimulus. It's a bit like when your teeth are overly sensitive to cold or hot drinks. Your dentist will advise you to use a special toothpaste, which will gradually desensitize your teeth to the pain so that eventually you can drink hot and cold liquids without experiencing discomfort.

How does SDT work?

Reversal of our learning

SDT is a form of **behavioural therapy** and works by reversing learned behaviours. It does this by applying the principles of **classical conditioning**. This means that the fear response of the phobia is removed by substituting a relaxation response to the conditioned stimulus by a gradual means using counter-conditioning. Let us look at this in action by applying it to an example, of a person who is terrified of rats and who becomes extremely alarmed and distressed in their presence.

Murophobia/Musophobia

Fear of Rats

The treatment will involve taking the **conditioned stimulus** (**CS**) – the rat – and then inhibiting the usual **conditioned response** (**CR**) – the panic. This is achieved by means of an intervention known as **counter-conditioning** (a relaxation technique), which makes it difficult for the person to panic when confronted by the **CS** because they are now in a relaxed state. They will now be able to confront the rat in a much calmer manner (an **adapted response**).

If you recall from a previous chapter, it is biologically impossible to be in a state of acute arousal/panic while simultaneously being in a state of relaxation. Relaxation is incompatible with anxiety, therefore the relaxation response counters the fear and anxiety response. By inducing a state of relaxation by means of a relaxation technique, such as slow, measured breathing, we inhibit the firing off of the fight or flight response. Your Personal Protection Officers, the amygdalae, read the situation as non-threatening and thus the association of the (CS) rat and the (CR) panic are severed. The person is now free to fondle rats to their heart's desire!

Please note that what we have previously been referring to as the **phobic stimulus** has the same meaning as the **conditioned stimulus**.

Method used in SDT

The method used in this therapy is extremely simple and in a nutshell consists of five key steps, as follows:

1. Explore your fears
2. Learn relaxation techniques
3. Learn how to score your fears
4. Design a hierarchy of fears
5. Implement the hierarchy while using relaxation techniques.

1. Explore your fears

Discuss your fear with your therapist in as much detail as you can so that they can gain an overview as to the extent of your problem. Be specific about what exactly you are afraid of and the extent of the fear.

Scoliodentosaurophobia

Fear of Lizards

Nicky had a fear of geckos, but it was only the transparent ones that upset her. She found the sight of their internal organs extremely disturbing. If one appeared on the wall in her house in Trinidad she would scream and run out of the room in a panic and not be able to return until someone had removed it. Although she was not overly fond of lizards in general she felt reasonably comfortable in their presence and did not feel that they posed a problem for her – what she was specifically afraid of was seeing the internal organs in the transparent variety, and so her treatment had to be tailored to that end.

2. Learn relaxation techniques

With your therapist's help, or through self-training, you should learn relaxation techniques, which may involve breathing in a particular way, meditating, progressive muscle relaxation exercises or the use of guided visualization imagery.

Acrophobia

Fear of Heights

Angus had a fear of heights and dreaded attending the monthly board meeting, which was held on the sixteenth floor of his office. What particularly disturbed him was the coffee break in which refreshments were served in an area with a clear glass frontage where the panoramic view was unavoidable. He felt that it was impossible for him to not focus on the fact that he was so high up and would start to sweat and tremble and become increasingly distressed. So Angus applied the breathing techniques he had learned in therapy to keep himself calm. By consciously breathing in a slow, measured manner, using his entire abdomen, Angus was able to halt his shallow, thoracic breathing (see page 185), which was causing him to hyperventilate. As he gained more control he was able to ensure that his 'out' breath was slightly slower than his 'in' breath, which forced his body into the relaxation mode.

---

3. Learn how to score your fears

Learn how to grade or rate your fear/anxiety level between one and ten by thinking about a situation in which you feel totally comfortable and relaxed that might give you a score of one, e.g. enjoying a bubble bath. Then think about a situation that might give you a score of nine or ten, e.g. encountering a snake in the dark when you are all alone. You will then be able to give numerical values to a number of situations for your fear hierarchy.

Gephyrophobia
Fear of Crossing Bridges

Bex described being totally relaxed whilst enjoying a barbecue in the garden of her girlfriend's house in the Welsh Valleys. She scored this as a one. Her worst fear, which she scored as a ten, was the idea of driving on a long, exposed bridge over water. She said that she was terrified by the thought that she might panic and lose complete control of her car.

---

4. Design a hierarchy of fears

Brainstorm a series of situations which you would find upsetting with regard to your phobia and write them down on Post-it notes. You then give each of these notes a score between one and ten in terms of your level of fear. Having given each a score, arrange them in ascending order with those with the lowest score on the bottom and the most feared situation on the top. This is known as your hierarchy of fears. Some people like to present this as a pyramid with the most difficult challenge at the summit, while other people prefer to present this in reverse by putting the easiest challenge at the top and the most anxiety-provoking challenge at the bottom.

It is important to ensure that you have a range of situations from low (mildly anxiety-provoking) to high (intensely anxiety-provoking) scores. If a jump is too great, say from a level three score to a six, you might well lose confidence so keep in mind the theme of *gradually confronting* your fear.

Equinophobia
Fear of Horses

Frank had a fear of horses, which he had largely managed to avoid since he lived in the city. His company had decided to relocate to the countryside and had purchased a property located close to a stud farm. When visiting the new site Frank was dismayed to discover that he could not avoid passing a paddock of horses in order to access his office. Realizing that it was now imperative that he address his phobia he designed the hierarchy of fears below (you can find an alternative hierarchy of fears for Claustrophobia in the appendix on page 205).

Hierarchy of Fears

Looking at drawings of horses	1
Saying the word 'horse' out loud	1
Looking at photographs of horses	2
Looking at a model of a horse	3
Imagining holding the model of the horse	3
Holding a model of a horse	4
Watching a film about horses	5
Driving past a field of horses	6
Imagining looking at a horse at close quarters	6
Getting out of the car to watch the horses	7
Calling a horse over and watching it at close quarters	8
Imagining reaching out to feed a horse	8
Reaching out with some carrots to feed a horse	9
Imagining touching a horse	9
Stroking a horse	10

5. Implement the hierarchy while using relaxation techniques

Design and execute a plan in which you incrementally work your way through your hierarchy of fears until you get to the end. As you approach each situation you apply your relaxation techniques and repeat the experience until you can comfortably handle the situation. You may have to do this several times before you move on to negotiate the next level. It is important to be sure that you have confidently achieved a level before moving on, otherwise you might find yourself avoiding the next task since the jump up in the fear stakes feels too great.

You should never progress to the next level until you can perform the current task in a relaxed manner. **Slow but sure is the way to go**, rather than rushing yourself and then having to regress to a lower level. Remember that people have often lived with a phobia for a considerable amount of time, so investing a few extra days or weeks to ensure that it is eradicated properly is time well spent.

Progress is seldom linear

Sometimes you may have to retrace earlier stages anyway, since how we negotiate our hierarchy of fears is also contingent upon other things going on in our life. For example, you may have had a poor night's sleep and be feeling exhausted and fretful. It would not be sensible to move up to another level at this point, since your anxiety levels are already in a heightened state. It would be far better to consolidate your previous success by practising at your current level or return to an even lower level despite the fact that you had planned to move up to another level that day.

The main thing is to not be disheartened and accept

that sometimes we need to take a step back before moving forwards. Setbacks are a fundamental part of trying to learn a new way of doing things. They are just small bumps in our path to change and should not derail us from continuing with our progress. Remember that to falter is not the same as failing; faltering is a normal component of most change patterns.

Be prepared to adjust tasks

You might find that you struggle with a particular level for some time; if so, it might be sensible to make it easier by breaking the task down into more manageable components. You can do this by asking someone to do the task first, while you watch. This way you will have visual evidence that the situation is not as dangerous as you were anticipating. This is known as **modelling**, since by witnessing someone else in the presence of the phobic stimulus responding with relaxation and not fear you will be able to copy or imitate their behaviour. For example, you might watch someone else stroke a pet rabbit before you attempt to do so yourself.

Another way you can make a task more manageable is by calling on the support of someone else to accompany you first before you attempt the task on your own. For example, you might be struggling to go up to the third floor in a lift on your own, having successfully managed to get to the second floor solo. You could ask someone to accompany you from floor two to three to enable you to gradually build up your confidence by having their support initially and then attempt it on your own.

Feel free to make changes to your hierarchy

Sometimes when we are designing our hierarchy we can make mistakes in the weighting which we give to each task, finding that some work out to be too easy and some too hard. It is not a problem to adjust them accordingly and even add in new situations or remove ones that you feel are inappropriate in the light of your current progress. The main thing is to treat it like an experiment and be prepared to be flexible.

Concrete evidence that your fear is not justified

The important concept to grasp about how this treatment works is that by staying in each feared situation long enough for our anxiety levels to drop, we gain the experiential knowledge that the fear is not justified. Although at an intellectual level we would have already known this to be the case, we would now have cast-iron evidence that we can both tolerate and survive in the feared situation without having to experience overwhelming symptoms of anxiety/panic. The more we repeat a level the more confident we will become.

This works in exactly the same way that we increase our confidence with regard to exam performance. The more that we revise the topics upon which we are to be tested the more confident we become that we can deliver the right response in the actual exam. The brain picks up this increased confidence and composure and new templates will be formed, overwriting the current existing patterns that previously evoked the panic response.

Systematic Desensitization is not the only form of exposure therapy, and in the next chapter we will look at other forms which can be offered for the treatment of phobias.

12. Types of Exposure, Flooding and Implosion

Imaginal Exposure

It is often an excellent idea to do what is known as **imaginal exposure** as a way of making a task more manageable. This is where we explore the feared situation in our imagination first before confronting it for real. We can do this either on our own or with the help of a therapist who will describe a feared scenario in graphic detail whilst we apply our relaxation techniques. This is known as a **visualization technique**.

 Try to imagine experiencing your phobia. For example, if you have a fear of going on a boat, use your imagination to explore how it might feel to be on a long voyage on a rough sea with the boat pitching and tossing in the waves. How does this make you feel?

In vivo exposure

When we do the task for real, as in taking a trip on a boat or visiting a zoo to encounter a snake, this is referred to as **in vivo exposure**. The literal translation of this Latin expression is 'within the living'. Incidentally, there are several zoos that offer special programmes specifically for people who wish to overcome their fear of spiders or snakes. The bene-fit of this form of exposure is that by actually physically confronting your fear in the real situation you will have no doubts whatsoever that you have overcome your phobia.

Virtual exposure

There is also a third form of exposure, which is known as **virtual exposure**. This is where technological aids such as simulators are used to produce a lifelike experience in which the client can be exposed to their feared situation. For example, virtual reality helmets can be used for someone who has a fear of driving through a tunnel. The therapist can monitor the sufferer's pulse rate and stop the experi-ence from time to time by freezing the frame in order to implement relaxation techniques if the person is becoming too distressed.

It is worth mentioning that purely by using imaginal or virtual exposure many people are able to overcome their phobia completely. This of course is excellent news for situations where it would be impractical or prohibitively expensive to conduct an in vivo exposure session.

For example, this method is often used for people who have a fear of thunderstorms, as it is difficult to organize in vivo exposure due to the vicissitudes of the weather. Equally, sometimes the need for anonymity and privacy for public figures makes this method more appealing. Finally, this method affords total personal safety as the experience can be stopped if the sufferer loses control. This makes it an excellent choice for those who have a fear of heights. For those with a fear of driving, they can build up their confidence without putting themselves or other road users at risk.

Summary of SDT

Systematic Desensitization is a form of therapy that enables you to unlearn negative associations which you have learnt, such as that jellyfish (CS) cause fear and panic (CR). It does this by introducing relaxation strategies, which actively compete with your anxiety. By being in your feared situation in a much calmer frame of mind, due to the benefits of the relaxation techniques, you then gain sound proof that the feared situation is not threatening or dangerous.

The following forms of exposure therapy are *not* conducted in this gradual, incremental manner.

Flooding or implosion

Some of you may have heard of other forms of **exposure therapy**, known as **flooding** or **implosion**. These forms of therapy are not for the faint-hearted since they involve the person with the phobia being exposed to their worst fear immediately.

Total instant immersion

This is rather like being asked to go straight to the most anxiety-provoking situation of your hierarchy of fears, at the very top of your pyramid. This form of therapy can be effective but it is extremely distressing for the sufferer since they will experience seriously intense levels of fear and anxiety. An example of this therapy in action would be if someone had a fear of spiders. Without further ado, they would be locked in a dark cellar full of spiders for an hour (or until they stopped screaming).

The way that this therapy works is that by rapidly exposing the person to their worst fear and preventing their escape from the situation two things are achieved. Firstly, the **avoidance response** is prevented, since the person cannot escape. Secondly, there is a deconditioning of the habit of experiencing panic when exposed to the phobic stimulus, due to the person becoming too exhausted to panic.

Panic burns itself out

As you will recall, the panic state (short-term survival mode) cannot be maintained indefinitely and will eventually stop and return to normal (long-term survival mode), even if the stimulus is still present. Because of the high level of energy expenditure needed to fuel the panic attack, the sufferer will scream and cry to the point of exhaustion. They will then, having worn themselves out in the feared situation, have to face the reality that nothing dreadful has happened to them and the danger was not as they had originally thought. The spiders did not gobble them up and they did not die of terror.

THINK ABOUT IT

Basophobia

Fear of Falling

As I said earlier, this treatment is not everyone's cup of tea and many practitioners feel ethically very uncomfortable about conducting exposure sessions that cause this level of distress. Many phobia sufferers dismiss it out of hand, convinced that they would have a heart attack if they were to be exposed to their worst fear in such a callous fashion.

As I am sure you will appreciate, this **non-gradual** approach to extinguishing a fear is very scary indeed. It would be like jumping straight off the five-metre board at the swimming baths without first having had the opportunity to acclimatize yourself to the one-metre and three-metre boards, if you suffered from a fear of falling.

Effective and fast, but can also be risky

On the plus side, this form of treatment is frequently effective and very efficient in terms of time and cost savings compared with other approaches. However, there is a very serious possible downside in that this approach has been known to backfire and leave the client worse off than they started, by traumatizing them further.

13. Cognitive Behavioural Therapy (CBT)

Cognitive Behavioural Therapy is one of the most popular current ways of treating phobias.

Cognitive refers to anything involving mental processes such as awareness, reasoning, perceiving, judging and thinking.

Behavioural simply refers to what we do, our actions and behaviours.

In a nutshell **CBT** examines how the way we *think* influences how we *feel* and ultimately how we *behave*.

 It is not our experiences in life which are the problem; it is our interpretation of those experiences that causes us difficulties.

This form of therapy is a happy marriage between Cognitive Therapy, Rational Emotive Therapy and Behaviourism and incorporates aspects of all three approaches. The pioneering work of luminaries such as Aaron Beck, Albert Ellis, Donald Meichenbaum and many others have all contributed to this blended form of treatment.

A popular approach

One of the reasons why CBT is so popular is because of all the psychological approaches available, it is the one with the greatest body of scientific research to back it up. It has been compared with many other forms of treatment, including medication, and has fared very well in the various trials and studies. In Britain, the NHS has invested a considerable amount of money in the training of CBT practitioners to enable this form of treatment to be more widely available to the public.

Another reason why it is held in high regard is because it teaches people how to constructively challenge themselves when they are confronted with difficulties and problems. These tools have universal application and therefore, having learned the techniques, people can apply these skills to future problems and be in a position to help themselves.

Overview

The treatment largely consists of challenging dysfunctional emotions, maladaptive behaviours and the beliefs that are causing upset and disturbance. New practical skills are then developed to enable the person to manage their life more positively by eliminating previous symptoms and vulnerabilities which have held them back in the past.

The new strategies are then put to the test by applying systematic desensitization or other behavioural techniques. The essence of the approach is the belief that our responses to the world are a result of a complex interaction between our *thoughts*, *feelings* and *behaviours*.

Before we look at CBT further I have included a couple of examples that illustrate this important link between our **thoughts** (that is, what we believe is happening), how those thoughts affect how we then **feel** and as a consequence how we then **behave**.

My late and much beloved grandmother, Isabella, used to say after she had eaten her meal with gusto and her plate was completely bare, 'I didn't enjoy that much'. All of her family knew immediately that this was her way of saying that she had thoroughly appreciated her supper. I distinctly remember an occasion when a friend, who had joined us that evening, looked incredibly confused and embarrassed on hearing my grandmother's remark. As a result of her discomfort, my friend became a little subdued. She later confided that she thought my grandmother was a real stoic, in that she had polished off to the last bite a meal that she had found distasteful. My friend, being oblivious to my grandmother's sense of humour, had clearly taken the literal meaning, not appreciating that the comment was intended as a compliment to the chef.

As you can see from this simple example, we often get things totally wrong. Our interpretation of events, what we **think** is happening, will have a direct influence on how we **feel** about the situation, in my friend's case, bewilderment and embarrassment. These feelings in turn caused her to **behave** in a subdued manner.

The impact of the above was neither here nor there, however, sometimes our incorrect interpretation can cause us much pain and anguish. A glaring example that springs to mind is one that I constantly meet in my work with people who have a fear of flying. This is over the phenomenon of turbulence, a perfectly normal and natural part of flying but sadly misinterpreted by so many as life-threatening.

Aviophobia

Fear of Flying

In this case study I will outline the thoughts, feelings and behaviour of two people on board an aircraft who experience exactly the same **objective reality**, this being mild turbulence. However, their **subjective reality** is very different due to the **beliefs** which they hold. The pilot, Alona, by virtue of her role, has greater experience and knowledge of this phenomenon and therefore has the more accurate perspective of the two.

Our passenger, Bruce, a businessman, has his own, albeit erroneous, perspective on turbulence. This has been crafted and honed over the years, by his relentless absorption of a steady diet of Hollywood flight disaster movies. Unsurprisingly, Bruce is now not a happy flier, having indoctrinated himself that flying is a perilous pursuit. Occasionally Bruce has to fly because of his work. He does this with tremendous reluctance, since he dare not jeopardize his employment by refusing. Providing he doesn't encounter turbulence, Bruce feels he can just about get through the flight.

Conflicting interpretations of turbulence
Alona, the pilot, experiences turbulence and we get the following responses:

Thinks: *I know that turbulence is totally safe, but I think that I'll switch the seatbelt signs on. Sadly this will delay the meal service but I know it's for the best since I don't want to risk passengers having drinks spilled onto their laps. I will check to see if I can fly at a different altitude so as not to inconvenience the passengers who are probably hungry, particularly those who have skipped breakfast because of the early check-in time.*

Feels: Totally calm and relaxed, but a little concerned that the passengers are probably feeling hungry and the cabin crew will be rushed to complete the meal service if the delay is too long.

Behaves: Switches the seatbelt sign on and checks the route to see if she can adjust the flight path so that the meal service is not too badly delayed.

Bruce the businessman experiences turbulence and we get the following responses:

Thinks: *Here we go – seatbelt signs have been switched on. Oh my goodness, we've hit turbulence, it's so dangerous,* *let's hope that the wings don't snap off. I should never have got into this contraption in the first place, they're death traps. Whoever is up there, you have got to get me down. I need a triple whisky to steady my nerves but they can't serve me because of this wretched turbulence. If it ever stops I'm going to drink the bar dry. What on earth is wrong with this chap next to me? He's laughing his head off at some film or other whilst we're going through hell and fighting for our lives, he must be some sort of halfwit. Oh my stars, I'm having a panic attack, I can hardly swallow and I'm struggling to breathe. Crikey, my heart is beating so irregularly. I know what this means, I'm on the verge of having a heart attack. I hope that my family manages to find my will since I hid it in my underpants drawer. Did I remember to kiss my wife, children and dog before I left this morning and did I tell them that I love them? Confound that maniac next to me, he's finished his show and has started to read his newspaper, what the blazes is wrong with him, doesn't he know that we're all going to die?*

Feels: Initially extremely anxious, then unbearably alarmed, followed by utterly petrified.

Behaves: Fastens his seatbelt instantly and pulls it so tight that he risks dismembering himself. Stretches his neck like a meerkat and swivels his head around trying to locate a member of the cabin crew. Spots a stewardess and stares penetratingly into her eyes, scrutinizing them for signs of impending doom. Does the white-knuckle ride by gripping on to the armrests of his seat. Prays frantically to the gods of all the religions he can muster up. Frowns incredulously at the guy beside him who is thoroughly enjoying the in-flight entertainment, seemingly totally oblivious of the current danger, but nonetheless will reap the benefit of his prayers should the gods be minded to spare the aircraft. Hyperventilates, trembles and sweats profusely. Clutches his chest, emitting grunts and groans while doing so. Most importantly, pledges that he will avoid flying for the rest of his life if he manages to get down in one piece.

Phobias are based on irrational beliefs with regard to threat

The above shows that by misinterpreting a situation as a result of holding incorrect beliefs, people can suffer unbearable distress. People with phobias invariably hold incorrect beliefs with regard to the **real** threat level of their **phobic stimulus**.

Bruce's return home and therapy

Let us now look at this form of treatment in a bit more detail – we can use our businessman's experience to help anchor the theory in to practice. Incidentally Bruce did land safely but sadly missed his meeting due to having got himself into a drunken state at the hotel and then falling asleep.

Bruce made it back home using overland transport, incurring extra costs for his company. His boss, Oliver, told him kindly but firmly that if he wanted to keep his current position he would need to be able to fly. Alternatively, he could accept a demotion to a role where overseas travel was not required but that would result in a serious reduction in his salary. Bruce promised to give his situation some thought and would come to his decision within a week. Oliver was an enlightened boss and said that if he did decide to confront his fear of flying, he knew of an excellent CBT therapist who had helped several other members of staff over the years.

Method of treatment

Cognitive Behavioural Therapy consists of five key stages, which are used to help a person overcome their phobia. You will find a form on page 145 that a practitioner would use to help a client to explore their problem. At the top of the page you will see the letter **A**, where the *Activating Event* is identified. Below this line there are four columns labelled **B**, **C**, **D** and **E**, which is where *Beliefs, Consequences, Dispute beliefs and Enact/Experiment* respectively are recorded.

Stages of treatment

1. Psychological assessment (A, B, C)
2. Reconceptualization of the phobia (D)
3. Acquisition of new skills (D)
4. Application of new skills and reconceptualization (E)
5. Maintenance of new frame of reference (E)

Stage 1

Psychological assessment

In stage one the extent of the problem is assessed and the *Activating Event* is recorded on the form under section **A**. In the **B** column, the details of the *Beliefs* held by the client about the event are then recorded. In the **C** column, the *Consequences* of the beliefs will be listed. This will involve recording both emotions and behaviours.

Stage 2

Reconceptualization of the phobia

This is the stage when the practitioner and client work together to dispute or challenge the original beliefs and formulate new, more rational, beliefs to put in their place. Along with amending the client's beliefs they will also discuss the ways in which they can implement the new beliefs, by putting them into action. This is done by:

1. Comparing evidence that supports and refutes the current erroneous belief and as a consequence of this information updating how the client now interprets the situation, known as *reconceptualization*.

2. Exploring cognitive distortions in the client's thinking process (see list of cognitive distortions in chapter 14).

3. Planning how the client will confront their fear in the future – an exposure hierarchy will usually be designed at this stage.

All of the above would be recorded under the **D** section on the form.

Stage 3

Acquisition of new skills

During this stage the client will be taught relaxation strategies which will help them to cope more calmly when confronted with their fear while executing stage 4. These strategies may consist of breathing exercises or guided visualization techniques. These new strategies will be recorded in the **D** column on the form.

Stage 4

Application of new skills and reconceptualization

In this fourth stage the client is ready to enact or put into practice their amended beliefs while applying their newly acquired relaxation skills. Having worked on their cognitive distortions, the client will be more rational in how they evaluate the various experiences as they work their way up their hierarchy of fears. These activities or experiments will be recorded in section **E** on the form along with the new consequences, i.e. emotions and behaviours.

A: Activating event			Date:
B: Beliefs (Images/Attitudes/Meaning/Rules)	**C:** Consequences (Behaviours/Actions)	**D:** Dispute (Evidence/Cognitive Distortions/Relaxation Strategies)	**E:** Enact/Experiment (New Consequences/Behaviours/Emotions)

Stage 5

Maintenance of new frame of reference

The final stage is where the client, having accomplished the various tasks by successfully reaching the top of their fear hierarchy, now ensures that they maintain what they have achieved. In order to not lapse back into a phobia or develop a new problem it is important to maintain a healthy, well-balanced lifestyle. It is also helpful to periodically revisit the forms, which were completed while addressing the phobia. Column **E** will offer concrete written evidence showing how you were able to cope with your fear and will prove to be an excellent reminder of your capability. Finally it is also advisable to keep on your toes with regard to checking for new cognitive distortions. By continuing to scrutinize the way that we think, we can avoid slipping back into unhealthy thinking habits.

In practice, the way this works is as follows: If someone had the cognitive distortion of catastrophizing (see page 160) and suffered from a phobia of public speaking, they would be encouraged to challenge their belief that if they dried up while addressing their colleagues at a meeting it would be the end of the world (amend belief). They would apply their relaxation techniques (new skills) and tell themselves that if they do become tongue-tied then their colleagues are actually far more likely to be sympathetic than to ridicule them (reconceptualization). This reframing of the situation will produce very different feelings and behaviours, which will then be duly recorded. They will then be able to look at this empirical evidence to see that what they feared did not happen, or if it did then it was not as unbearable as their catastrophic thinking had anticipated.

Applying the method to Bruce

Bruce wisely decided that he wanted to sort out his problem. He reckoned that he used to quite like flying before he went through that addictive phase of watching airline horror movies. He enjoyed his career and didn't fancy the other job or the financial consequences so he sought the help of Georgina, a CBT practitioner.

Georgina helped Bruce to explore his problem by using the simple ABC Model discussed above. You can see how the questions applied to Bruce below:

A – The activating event was the onset of turbulence

B – The beliefs/thoughts. Here are some of Bruce's thoughts:

'Turbulence is dangerous and I won't be able to stand the situation since I think that I will have a panic attack and a heart attack and am very likely to die.'

C – The consequences
Bruce had experienced very unpleasant physical sensations including panic symptoms as well as very distressing

emotions such as anxiousness, anger, helplessness and fearfulness. He had also expressed his determination not to fly again but had obviously reconsidered due to the potential impact on his employability and the inevitable upset for his family who relished their holidays abroad.

D – Dispute the irrational beliefs and thoughts

Alternative explanations: Georgina asked Bruce to think about his last flight and see if he could come up with some other explanations about his experience with turbulence.

Relaxation techniques: Georgina also discussed a number of techniques that Bruce could use to try to remain calm when confronting his fears. (You will find some relaxation exercises you can try in chapter 16.)

Cognitive distortions: Most importantly she explained to Bruce about a number of bad habits we can fall into with regards to our thinking process and how they can lead to irrational thoughts. (We will look at these 'cognitive distortions' in the next chapter, as they are important.)

Below are some of the alternative ideas Bruce came up with during his session.

'When I think about it, where is the evidence that turbulence is dangerous?'

'Does the crew come to work each day unsure if they are ever going to see their families again should they hit a bit of turbulence during the flight? It doesn't really sound very plausible.'

'Do aircraft wings really snap off because of turbulence? Come to think of it nobody's ever heard of it happening in real life, but I have seen it at the movies …'

'What other ways could I look at the situation, which might be more realistic? Hmm, well thinking about it, I am now beginning to wonder if that guy I was sitting next to was really nuts. Maybe he was behaving in that unconcerned manner because there was nothing really to be concerned about, apart from the fact that I needed a drink and couldn't b----y get one.'

'Perhaps you can no more expect to have a turbulence-free flight every time that you fly than you can expect the ocean to be always like a mill pond when you go sailing.'

'But what about the panic attack I experienced? I didn't have any control over that. But then I suppose that I didn't have the most healthy attitude towards turbulence in the first place, and I guess that's what wound me up.'

'Those chest pains were terrifying. I had convinced myself that I was dying. I don't want to have to repeat that experience again in a hurry. So yes, I'm certainly up for trying out those guided visualization techniques so that I can keep myself calm.'

'I like the sound of the slow breathing exercises, they'll come in handy. Do you know that I often hyperventilate when I get in a tizzy about things?'

E – Enact new learning and skills – experiment

Georgina then discussed ways in which Bruce could experiment with his new skills and more rational thinking style by putting them into practice. Bruce was to keep a journal and record his thoughts and feelings, together with the evidence accrued from his various experiences listed below in his hierarchy of fears. This way he could look back at his journal and see that what he had feared did not actually happen. Or if something he feared did actually happen, such as turbulence, he would have the evidence that he had been able to cope with his anxiety differently as a result of his new way of thinking and the application of relaxation skills.

Together they worked out a hierarchy of feared flying experiences, starting with the least anxiety-provoking and culminating in the situation which Bruce feared the most. With Georgina's support, Bruce worked through this hierarchy until he was at last able to fly confidently on his own on long-haul flights.

Hierarchy of fears

Imagine a visit to the airport	1
Accompanied visit to the airport	1
Visit to the airport unaccompanied	2
Read a book in which turbulence is explained	2
Imagine taking a short flight	2
Listen to a guided visualization of a flight	3
Experience a session in a flight simulator	4
Take an accompanied short domestic flight	5
Do the return sector with support person in another row	6
Take a short flight on your own	7
Take an accompanied intermediate length flight	8
Do the return sector with support person in another row	8
Take an intermediate flight on your own	9
Take an accompanied long-haul flight	9
Do the return sector with support person in another row	9
Take a long-haul flight on your own	10

Having seen how CBT works by exploring Bruce's fear of flying, we are now going to look at cognitive distortions or thinking errors in the next chapter, since they play such a key role in causing irrational behaviour.

14. Cognitive Distortions

If you recall, one of the hallmarks of a phobia is that your fear is irrational. That is, your evaluation of the magnitude of the threat is plain wrong. The threat either doesn't exist at all or you have blown it up out of all proportion. Since this is the case, it makes abundant sense to look at your cognitive style in some detail. By this I am referring to how you tend to think, perceive and reason. In this chapter we will explore in a little more depth how people think, since this is what gets them into trouble with a phobia in the first place.

Do you think sensibly?

If what you do is a result of how you feel, which has been caused by how you think, then you had better ask yourself this question: are you thinking sensibly, or irrationally? If the answer is the latter then it is time to have a rethink, since it will probably mean that you are behaving irrationally as a result.

How can we make our thoughts more rational?

Many of us are of the opinion that we have no control over our thoughts, but this is far from the case. Thoughts, like behaviours, are just creatures of habit. In the same way that we can break a negative behavioural habit, we can equally break a destructive thinking habit.

For instance, after many episodes of wasting an inordinate amount of time searching the house for my car keys, I have retrained myself to put them in a specific place each time I finish using them. This was such a simple solution but I admit that it did take me a bit of time before it melded into my DNA; now my new habit is so proficient, I do it on autopilot.

THINK ABOUT IT

What examples can you think of from your own life where a bit of rational thought could solve a problem?

How to change behaviour

How did I change my car key habit? First of all I had to acknowledge that it was counterproductive and not serving me well, since it had caused me to be late a few times. Secondly, I took a very conscious decision that I wanted to change this bad habit. Thirdly, I designed a more useful habit that I wanted to adopt, that is, putting them in a specific place as soon as I entered the house. Fourthly, whenever I found that I had lapsed, by discovering my keys when I unpacked my handbag upstairs, I forced myself to address my error, no matter how inconvenient. I would instantly traipse down the stairs and restore my keys to their allotted parking receptacle. Eventually my brain realized that it was a bore to have to do this and therefore started to remember automatically. And hey presto, I had developed a new constructive behaviour!

I am sure that you all have been riveted by this thrilling example, but I felt that it was important to labour the point with regards to the process of changing a habit. This is because changing negative thinking habits is just as laborious as changing negative behavioural habits, and requires the same degree of dedication if we are to eliminate cognitive distortions. Incidentally, I am currently working on changing my bad habit of not filing away papers after I have finished with them. This is a work in progress as evidenced by the current state of my study floor!

 Now let's look at a simple example that shows our dominant way of thinking.

Look at the questions below and for each, choose the response that most closely matches the type of thoughts that you tend to entertain.

1. **An acquaintance tells you that the colour you are wearing really suits you. You think:**

   (a) 'Oh, I'm glad she thinks so because that's what I thought when I chose it.'

   (b) 'She's just being polite and she probably thinks it looks horrible.'

   (c) 'I wonder what she is after ...?'

2. **Your company is offering an incentive scheme, which will mean a financial bonus will be awarded to the top three performers. You think:**

   (a) 'Gosh, how exciting, I work pretty hard anyway but it will be great to gain that extra bit of cash by really going for it.'

   (b) 'Well I have no chance of getting into the top three. Let's hope that they don't start publishing our sales figures because I'll probably come bottom.'

   (c) 'Oh yeah, must be some sort of gimmick so that they can freeze our pay and not have the unions on to them. Besides, knowing that lot in management it will all be rigged anyway.'

3. **You wake up to a glorious sunny day. You think:**

   (a) 'Brilliant, what a fabulous day, I must get some friends together after work and have a barbecue.'

   (b) 'Oh dear, it's going to be roasting at work being cooped up all day in this heat.'

   (c) 'Typical, just got back from the wettest holiday ever and the sun decides to shine because yours truly is back at work today. No doubt we'll have to pay for this sunshine at the weekend when I'm meant to be at an open-air concert.'

4. **Your friend borrowed £100 and has called round to return the money. She hands it to you in an envelope. When she has gone you open the envelope and find that it is £10 short. You think:**

   (a) 'She must have made a mistake, it's easily done. I'll give her a call and she can give me the rest when I see her on Friday.'

   (b) 'I guess that I'll have to kiss goodbye to my £10 since it would be so embarrassing to tell her that the money was short, plus she probably wouldn't believe me anyway.'

   (c) 'Yeah right, does she think she's getting away with that? I didn't come down in the last shower; wait till I see her, she'll soon enough learn that she can't pull a fast one on me.'

5. **You have been invited to a ball by a local dignitary. You think:**

   (a) 'How thrilling, that's so kind of him to invite me and I'm really looking forward to going. I wonder which outfit I should wear? I think that I'll treat myself to a visit to the hairdresser's, since it's such a smart occasion."

   (b) 'Oh no, I'm dreading it. I know that he only asked because he feels sorry for me or didn't feel it would look right if I was the only one left out. I'll probably look out of place and be left on my own all evening unless someone takes pity and comes to talk to me.'

(c) 'I know his type, bet there's some hidden agenda, there's no such thing as a free lunch. He's probably raising funds for something or other and expecting us to fork out when we get there.'

So how did you get on? Were your thoughts/responses generally As, Bs or Cs? Perhaps you were inclined to be the optimistic A character? Or were you the rather pessimistic B sort? Or maybe you are of a cynical disposition and opted for the C category? I know that these questions were lacking in subtlety but I wanted to make the point that we do have habitual ways of thinking about the world and how we interact within it.

Does your style of thinking serve you well?

Being stuck in habitual ways of thinking is not always constructive, especially if our thoughts have a tendency to be irrational. It doesn't take a genius to work out which of our three characters, above, is most likely to find their interactions with people, and life in general, the most positive and engaging. Even if A were accused of being overly optimistic and cheerful, at least they are having fun being that way, whereas B seems to almost be apologizing for living and C's caustic cynicism would make most people head for the hills.

Thinking errors lead to irrational thoughts

Just in case you need to be reminded, phobias are irrational fears and therefore we need to root out our irrational thoughts and expose them for the imposters that they are. **Irrational thoughts** can usually be attributed to the common mistakes listed below. As I've mentioned before, they are often referred to as cognitive distortions. As you read through the explanations, make a note of your score by the heading in accordance with the table below:

1. Never think this way   score 0
2. Seldom think this way   score 1
3. Frequently think this way   score 2
4. Usually think this way   score 3

The ten deadly sins of thinking

1. Catastrophizing
2. Musterbating
3. Personalizing
4. Filtering
5. Monochromatic thinking
6. Extrapolating
7. Intolerant thinking
8. Emotional thinking
9. Mind-reading
10. Pessimistic thinking

1. Catastrophizing

Catastrophizing, a term coined by Albert Ellis, is when we inflate a situation negatively. The expression we use is, 'to make a mountain out of a molehill'. If you are about to entertain your boss and her husband and you are unable to buy the recommended type of mushrooms for the risotto, do you hear yourself saying things like:

'That's completely ruined the menu, the dinner party is going to be a total disaster, my boss is going to think that I am completely inept and will certainly not offer me that promotion I was hoping for – in fact I might even lose my job if she thinks that I am this useless.'

If you tend to think like this it is important that you stop yourself and learn to put things into perspective, termed 'decatastrophizing', instead of leaping to the worst possible conclusion. Having an attitude like this is self-defeating and will make you less confident and resourceful. It is also irritating for those around you since nobody likes a drama queen. In reality it is highly unlikely that the world will stop spinning on its axis because you have the incorrect mushrooms. (That is, providing they are not poisonous!)

2. Musterbating

Musterbation is another term coined by Albert Ellis, the creator of Rational Emotive Behaviour Therapy (REBT). Ellis used this term to describe a style of thinking which is characterized by a high degree of **demandingness**. Another psychologist, Clayton Barbeau calls it 'should-ing yourself'.

Do you find yourself frequently thinking in phrases like, 'I **must** make a good impression', 'I **ought** to volunteer', 'I **should** make sure that I arrive early', 'I **have to** pass my test' or 'I **can't** be late'?

Equally, do you hear yourself thinking in this rigid way about others; 'they **shouldn't** drink so much', 'they **mustn't** lose this contract', 'they've **got to** apologize'? Finally, do you think 'life **should** be fair' and 'countries **should** never go to war' and 'all diseases **must** be eradicated'?

By holding rigid views about how you, others and the world **should** be, you are setting yourself up for disappointment, since we don't always get our own way. Soften the tone to a less extreme level and hold a more flexible approach. By rephrasing your demands into preferences, wants and wishes you would be more realistic. If you don't get your preferred outcome it will not feel like a total failure or disaster. For example, rephrase 'I must make them like me' to 'I would prefer them to like me', and change 'I have to pass my exam' to 'I want to pass my exam'.

3. Personalizing

Do you always jump to the conclusion that what is happening always has something to do with you? For example, if your team doesn't secure the contract that they were pitching for, do you then take the view that this failure must be down to the fact that your contribution was inadequate? Or if an acquaintance fails to acknowledge you in the street then do you imagine it must be because you have upset them in some way? By personalizing everything we fail to take into account all the other possibilities, such as that the acquaintance may not have seen you since they were not wearing their glasses. Or they didn't notice you because they were in another world with their thoughts.

By personalizing situations and jumping to the conclusion that something must be our fault, or invariably thinking that a general comment is really being directed at us, we land up taking responsibility for things that often have little to do with us. It is a waste of energy to carry guilt, which has a heavy emotional toll, for things we haven't done. Personalizing can also make us feel got at. A good example of this is the random checks that take place in airport security. When the beeper goes off, people can often feel singled out and victimized even though the selection is nothing personal. So in future, rather than automatically thinking 'it's all about me', try looking for alternative explanations for what is happening around you.

4. Filtering

Do you keep an open mind, or are you selective about what information you take in. For example, if you think that you are unpopular, do you only consider evidence that supports this view and ignore evidence that contradicts it. For instance would you tend to give great attention to not having been invited to a wedding but totally ignore the fact that your colleague has invited you to the theatre and a friend has asked you to a party?

People with negative filters tend to distort positive experiences. For example, if they had successfully passed a job interview they would swiftly brush this achievement aside by saying that they were only offered the job because very few people had bothered to apply.

These mental filters can really colour the way we see the world. I am sure that you are familiar with the term *'seeing the world through rose-tinted glasses'*. Having a positive bias can also make us slightly unrealistic, but it is far less damaging than filtering events through a negative lens.

So if you know that you are constantly seeking out evidence to support your view that you are incompetent, unattractive, inadequate, boring or unlucky then stop doing this because it's totally unrealistic and certainly not in your best interests. By filtering through biases we skew the truth. So try to ensure that your perspective on life is more balanced by not overlooking the positive factors.

People with social phobias tend to suffer from this cognitive distortion and filter out all available evidence that demonstrates that others are interacting with them in a pleasant manner. They will only notice the person who has ignored them and this in turn will reinforce their view that people find them boring or socially inadequate.

5. Monochromatic thinking

This is a very common cognitive distortion. Many of us are guilty of black and white thinking, where we view our world in 'all or nothing' terms. Everything is either fantastic or dreadful. The speech we made is either a triumph or a disaster, our boss is either fabulous or a psychopath, the film is a resounding success or a total flop.

Do you frequently find yourself talking in this polarized fashion? Real life does have different shades and it is important to recognize this fact, since few things are all good or all bad. The danger with taking this monochromatic approach is that unless we do something perfectly, which is seldom the case, we will immediately jump to the assumption it is a failure.

When we can learn to evaluate our achievements in a more realistic and measured manner by seeing the shades in between, we become more empowered. Rather than abject failure we can acknowledge partial success, which not only is realistic but serves to help us conserve our self-esteem and confidence.

6. Extrapolating

Do you have a tendency to extrapolate or over-generalize? When we make global deductions based on a single incident we are often incorrect. We have the saying that *'one swallow doesn't make a summer'* to caution us against this particular cognitive error.

For example, if at work you discover a mistake in a report which you have compiled, do you then rush to the conclusion that the rest of your work is probably riddled with errors too?

The danger with this way of thinking is that it can lead to stereotyping by turning single individual facts into supposedly universal truths. I think people with a phobia of dogs will be able to strongly identify with this particular cognitive bias. Often, based on a single bad experience with **ONE** dog they tend to over-generalize and reach the conclusion that **ALL** dogs are dangerous, resulting in the entire canine population being condemned in their eyes. Happily this belief is irrational and untrue since there are some lovely dogs out there (I share a home with one of them).

If you are prone to this unhealthy way of thinking, then learn to challenge your thoughts and ask yourself, 'Where is the evidence?' Just because one politician fiddles their expenses, it doesn't mean that they all do!

7. Intolerant thinking

Is the following type of thought familiar to you? 'I **can't stand** it when people rustle in the cinema' or 'being on a crowded tube train is **intolerable**' or 'I **can't bear** people who jump the queue'? By thinking in this way you inflate the problem and decrease your personal resources to deal with the difficulty. In fact you can tolerate a lot more than you give yourself credit for. By recognizing this reality it will enable you to handle situations far better and reduce your stress levels as a consequence.

So next time you hear yourself saying, 'I **can't stand** losing' or 'failing is **unbearable**', stop yourself and acknowledge that neither of these consequences are the end of the world and that you can tolerate them and survive. By thinking that we can't cope with a negative outcome we can land up procrastinating or avoiding things we really want to do. Don't let the mindset that you 'can't stand' the smell of hospitals prevent you from visiting a sick relative.

8. Emotional thinking

Your feelings are very important and can often serve you well when you are trying to reach a decision or form an opinion. However, they are not infallible and cannot compete with facts. Feelings are influenced by our imagination, previous experiences, physical health, degree of tiredness and other factors.

So if we're feeling paranoid it doesn't mean that people are tapping into our telephone conversations. Similarly if we are feeling invincible as a result of intoxication by drink or drugs it doesn't mean that it is OK to jump out of the window and try to fly.

Always pay attention to your feelings, but recognize that they may not be entirely accurate. You might feel that your boss has taken a dislike to you but if you can't back it up with concrete evidence that this is the case then don't rush off to hand in your resignation.

I have worked with a number of clients who have a constant feeling of foreboding that something dreadful is about to happen. By placing total reliance on their feelings alone they spend a great deal of their time in a very negative frame of mind. Feelings can be woefully unreliable, particularly if you are prone to worrying. You only have to look at people who have a phobia, since it is their incorrect emotional thinking which keeps them trapped in a false reality; a world where anything from bubble wrap to clouds can be seen as truly dangerous.

We can see emotional thinking in action with people who suffer from claustrophobia in particular. They feel that they will suffocate if they go through a tunnel or enter a telephone booth. Often accompanying the emotional feeling of being trapped are the feelings of losing control and the fear that they might attack someone in their bid to escape the incarceration.

9. Mind-reading

Are you guilty of using this expression when you are talking with other people: 'before you tell me, I know what you are going to say'? Apart from it being irritating to be on the receiving end of this expression, it is usually pretty inaccurate. In my work with clients I sometimes use a therapeutic tool known as transference. Put simply, this means that unconscious feelings that my client has for a significant person in their life are redirected onto me. I often hear phrases like, 'I know that you are disappointed in my progress', or, 'you are going to be really disgusted with me when I tell you what I have just done'. They tell me that I am going to be angry or pleased with them and attribute all manner of feelings, which are total news to me.

So if you have a tendency when talking to someone to

come to snap judgments about what they are thinking and feeling, such as that they are bored by you or feel superior to you, then try to limit this way of thinking. The point is, we don't know what other people are thinking and it usually is not in our best interest to make wild guesses. So if you spend time trying to mind-read then be prepared to accept the fact that it is not the most accurate form of communication and asking someone outright tends to be more reliable.

10. Pessimistic thinking

What you think about you'll bring about.
Anonymous

I have left this one until last since it is probably the worst cognitive distortion of them all. We only have to think about the well-known psychological concept of the self-fulfilling prophecy to appreciate the damage that this way of thinking can cause. If you are competing in a race and tell yourself that you are going to come last and disgrace your team, you will find that you have radically diminished your chances of winning. Equally if you were to psych yourself up that you are bound to fail your driving test or be jilted by your girlfriend then you are more than halfway towards bringing these eventualities about.

People who believe that by expecting the worst, things can only get better are right in a literal sense. However, what they fail to take into consideration is the fact that the brain works on expectations and to a great extent what we programme in is what we get out. So if you go to the youth club and think, 'I expect nobody will want to talk to me or be my friend', your body language will be giving off this very message.

The opposite of pessimistic thinking is positive thinking, which primes the person for success. It is far better to have the odd disappointment and not achieve something which you believed you could than to limit your chances in the first place by brainwashing yourself that you won't succeed anyway. Furthermore, by being a 'can do' type of person you will be more likely to have another go until you do succeed.

Your Cognitive Distortion Score

Having scored yourself on all ten types of cognitive distortion, add up your total score and see which range you fall into.

Cognitive Distortion Scores

0–5	Very healthy thinking style, providing that no one area has scored more than one.
6–12	OK thinking style, but need to focus on any areas where a two or more has been scored.
13–18	Suggest keeping a thought diary and try to work on each cognitive distortion scoring a two or above.
19–40	Suggest professional help to work through distortions with support.

Please note that even if your score is low but you score a three in any area, it might be helpful to seek professional help to address the problem.

In the next chapter, I will discuss my preferred approach to working with people suffering from a phobia.

15. My Preferred Approach

For many years I have worked with people with all types of phobias and use a very eclectic style of therapy. My preferred way of working is to facilitate an intense, short-term and highly pragmatic form of treatment. The actual choice of therapy is based on three key factors which are as follows:

1. The disposition of my client
2. The nature and seriousness of the phobia
3. The time available to deal with the problem.

I will now explain the above three factors in a bit more detail.

The disposition of my client

My client's disposition is crucial when working out a suitable treatment plan. Some people suddenly make up their mind that enough is enough and get the bit between their teeth and decide to deal with their problem 'balls out', to use an unsavoury but apposite phrase. These clients might even be prepared to opt for implosion therapy.

Other clients prefer a much slower pace and want to first understand *why* they have the problem, and then work in a more in-depth and incremental fashion. I frequently do accompanied flights with people who like to work in this fashion. They use the confidence gained by mastering a short domestic flight to spur them on to the next stage where they will attempt an intermediate flight. It is only by working their way gradually through their fears that they at last feel confident enough to attempt a long-haul flight.

Some other clients don't care in the slightest about why they have the problem and just want to acquire the necessary tools to deal with it so that they are no longer held back by their phobia.

The nature and seriousness of the phobia

Some people have very straightforward, specific phobias which only impact on their life to a limited degree. Others have more complex phobias that cause much greater hardship with regard to the quality of their daily lives. I am thinking along the lines of agoraphobia and social phobias, as opposed to a fear of crabs or reptiles. I am sure that you will readily appreciate that the former phobias are all-encompassing, whereas the latter are far easier to avoid and therefore do not impinge on an individual's daily life to the same extent.

Also, some people have phobias with other problems running alongside (described as co-morbidity) such as depression or obsessive-compulsive disorder (OCD). In these cases a more protracted and diverse treatment plan is often required. Sometimes the nature of the phobia lends itself to one form of treatment rather than another. For example, the treatment for a fear of water would be very different to how one would treat a fear of death – exposure therapy being appropriate for the former but definitely not the latter!

The time available to deal with the problem

If a client has to attend an interview on the twentieth floor of a high-rise tower block next week, my choice of treatment plan will be greatly curtailed as a result of the immediacy of the problem. Similarly, if someone attends one of my 'Flying with Confidence' courses, my choices as to suitable therapy are severely constrained by both time and the fact that it must be delivered to a large number of people simultaneously.

When I conduct these courses with individual clients, as a result of working on a one-to-one basis, I am able to tailor the therapy to suit my client's specific needs, so each course will be slightly different. Specializing in Hodophobia, which is a fear of travelling, I am often operating within very tight time frames. The old English expression that 'time and the tide waits for no man' is very appropriate when I am working with clients who have a fear of travelling by boat, but are due to embark on a cruise in ten days' time. In these instances the therapy applied will of necessity need to be short-term and work immediately.

Treatment plan

Bearing in mind the three constraints mentioned above, I would tailor a treatment plan to meet each individual client's needs. This could involve various combinations of

Cognitive Behavioural Therapy, Systematic Desensitization Therapy, Fast Rewind Technique, Human Givens Approach, Neurolinguistic Programming, Transactional Analysis and Person-Centred Therapy.

As mentioned earlier, it is not within the scope of this book to discuss all forms of treatment. I have covered the main approaches to phobia treatment, which are CBT and SDT. However, it is important for you to know that many different forms of treatment exist should you choose to seek professional support.

Sometimes when people have been deeply traumatized by an event, they might well need a specific intervention known as the Fast Rewind Technique, to enable them to confront their phobia. If you look under 'Useful Contacts' at the back of this book you will be able to find out more about this technique by going to the Human Givens website.

The approaches I use enable the client and me to achieve the following goals:

1. Promotion of the therapeutic alliance

2. Discovery of the likely origin of the problem

3. Establishment of the triggers for the phobic reaction

4. Detraumatization of the client

5. Elimination of unhealthy thinking patterns

6. Development of a new conceptualization of the problem

7. Provision of opportunities to put reconceptualization into practice.

4Rs Paradigm

Alongside the above, I also equip my clients with a very simple toolbox of skills, which I have called the 4Rs Paradigm, which enables them to deal with their anxiety/panic in the moment. So while the combinations of therapy listed above provide the backdrop of exploration and re-education to deal with the phobia, the 4Rs Paradigm provides the immediate, hands-on skills to enable the client to deal with the actual confrontation of their phobic stimulus.

I have used this simple formula with literally thousands of clients and have found it to be extremely effective. When I am working on a course for people who have the same phobia I often have over a hundred clients. The 4Rs Paradigm has enabled them to successfully confront their fear in the knowledge that they can employ these skills to cope with their anxiety and panic. In the next chapter we will look at the 4Rs Paradigm in detail, since I believe it to be fundamental for successfully overcoming anxiety and panic.

16. The 4Rs Paradigm

Body and mind impact on each other

It is not for nothing that we describe an irritating person as a 'pain in the neck', our weaknesses and vulnerability as our 'Achilles heel' or the relief or pleasure experienced when seeing something as a 'sight for sore eyes'. All of these expressions allude to the intimate link between mind and body.

The 4Rs Paradigm capitalizes on the indisputable fact that the body influences the mind and the mind influences the body. If our mind becomes anxious then our body becomes tense. If our body becomes relaxed then our mind too will calm down. In a sense the 4Rs Paradigm is a range of techniques that mechanically override the fight or flight response.

For people suffering from a phobia it is imperative that they learn how to override the fight or flight response since it is firing off inappropriately in a non-threatening situation. By intercepting this response before it is activated, or arresting it if the response is already underway, we are able to prevent ourselves from launching into or remaining in short-term emergency survival mode. This will then prevent the slew of uncomfortable symptoms that accompany this mode that tend to further fuel the panic, keeping the vicious cycle going.

Put another way, by sending signals to the brain that your breathing is slow and measured and your muscles are relaxed, we reassure the amygdalae that there is no current threat. They then settle down, the fight or flight response stops, stress hormones cease to be released and the 'thinking' part of the brain takes over and resumes normal long-term survival mode.

In a nutshell, now that you are no longer experiencing uncomfortable symptoms and have access to the thinking part of your brain, you will feel able to do what you planned to do in the first place. Such as get into the lift, take that train journey or deliver your speech.

The 4Rs simply stand for the following:

1. **React**
2. **Regulate**
3. **Relax**
4. **Rehearse**

The very good news about the 4Rs Paradigm is that not only does it equip you with the tools to deal with your phobia, but these skills are universal and will enable you to cope with any anxiety-producing situation. We will now look at each of these in turn.

1. React
Take Control

> *Do not yield to misfortunes, but meet them*
> *on the contrary with fortitude.*
> Virgil

> *A good resolve will make any port.*
> Horace

The above quotations powerfully explain that if we want to achieve a definite purpose in life, which in this case is to overcome a phobia, it is imperative that we have determination and take action. Talking and thinking about it will never bring about our wishes and desires. What is always required is some form of action; otherwise the status quo will persist.

The sooner that action is taken the sooner your goals will be achieved.

Take direct action
Having decided that you will no longer choose to live under the gremlin's dominion, be prepared to take action immediately. I am sure that you will agree that it is far easier to calm a person down who is only slightly irritated rather than someone who is apoplectic with rage. The same goes for anxiety, the faster you nip it in the bud, the easier it is for a person to calm down and return to normality. If you

can learn to react to your anxiety symptoms the moment you identify their presence, then you will find that calming yourself will be far easier than if you wait until you're in the throes of a full-blown panic attack.

This is achieved by:

a) Developing your self-awareness
Learn to detect, at the earliest possible stage, any signs of anxiety, such as sweaty palms, slightly faster breathing patterns, being easily distracted and so on. Each person reacts to anxiety differently and you need to recognize the subtle or not so subtle changes in your body, thoughts, emotions and behaviours.

For example, when you start to get anxious do you experience fluttery sensations in your tummy, or does a headache start to develop? Do you find concentration difficult and read the same page of your book over and over again without extracting any meaning from the passage you have read? Do you start to feel vulnerable and insecure and experience a powerful sense of foreboding? Or do you find yourself pacing up and down like a tiger, unable to settle, or become totally inert and scarcely move? By learning to recognize the early symptoms of anxiety you will then be able to react at the first opportunity.

b) Application of refocusing technique
Twanging a rubber band which you have attached to your wrist is a very simple, yet effective technique you can use to stop your negative thoughts in their tracks. You can equally

just give yourself a pinch. The key is to cause yourself sufficient discomfort so that your brain refocuses its attention on the pain. During the split second you are registering pain, your negative thoughts will have been blown out of the water. You will then be able to seize the initiative and impose a new course of direction. So instead of relentlessly travelling down the path leading to acute anxiety and panic you can choose another route.

c) Say 'STOP' and repeat a positive affirmation
By saying '**Stop**' to yourself, followed by a positive affirmation, you will be sending a message to your gremlin that you have no intention of following its orders. The brain works on expectations. By stating to yourself in a clear manner that you are not following the usual course of action, that is, experiencing anxiety symptoms followed by avoidance, you send a powerful message to the brain that you are in charge and intend to do things differently.

Remember that one of the hallmarks of insanity is to keep repeating the same old pattern and expecting different results. You know exactly how your anxiety pattern turns out, so be determined to change the pattern to enable you to produce a different result. This is the first step towards breaking the anxiety cycle habit.

It is best to make up your own affirmation, because by personalizing it you will be able to make it more meaningful for your own unique situation. Suggested affirmations might look something like the following:

'I will no longer allow my irrational fear to limit my life.'

'I am a strong and capable person and will choose to do what I want to do.'

'I am determined to exercise real control over my choices and will not be dictated to by a silly little gremlin.'

 Develop your own positive affirmations that you can use in a crisis.

---

2. Regulate
Control your breathing

> *Feelings come and go like clouds in a windy*
> *sky. Conscious breathing is my anchor.*
> Thich Nhat Hanh

This fabulous quotation encapsulates the power of conscious breathing. Breathing is one of the very few bodily functions we can do both unconsciously and consciously. This ability is our ticket to enabling us to prevent or arrest a panic attack.

 It is impossible to be in a state of panic while at the same time being in a state of relaxation, and so it is impossible to panic while we are breathing in a slow, measured manner.

Breathing and our mental state

Breathing is intimately connected to our mental state and responds swiftly to changes in that mental state. When we are frightened and anxious we are likely to hyperventilate, which means we over-breathe. This is because the brain, believing that we are under threat, will signal to the body to be prepared for intense physical exertion to escape from the danger or fight it. To do this, it is necessary for the body to generate greater quantities of energy, and oxygen plays an essential role in this process.

Instant response

An easy way to witness this acceleration in breathing is to bang a drum or blow a whistle behind some unsuspecting person. The fright will cause an instant increase in both heart rate and speed of breathing. Often you will also witness their startled response as they gasp, jump and clutch their heart.

Constructive use of increased oxygen intake

If the extra oxygen is put to good use in producing greater amounts of energy, which is instantly deployed by running or fighting, the body will swiftly return to normality once the threat has been dealt with. However, if we are merely hyperventilating but remaining sedentary then we will start to feel very uncomfortable as our body becomes too alkaline due to the over-breathing. Furthermore, the rapid breathing will also be signalling to the brain that the threat still exists and so your body will continue to release a cocktail of stress hormones, which in turn will cause the physical symptoms we discussed earlier.

Bringing your breathing under control

Happily this sequence can also work in reverse. All that is required to bring the body out of short-term emergency survival mode and back to normality is to slow the breathing rate down. If the body is breathing in a slow, measured fashion, it is interpreted by the brain as a non-threatening situation and thus the release of stress hormones will cease. To do this I advocate **4/4 breathing**, which involves breathing in for the count of four and out for the count of four.

Rapid inducement of a state of relaxation

Furthermore, this reversal can be brought about even more swiftly if the 'out' breath is longer than the 'in' breath. This is because the 'in' breath is linked to the **sympathetic** branch of the **autonomic nervous system** and the out breath is linked to the **parasympathetic** branch. The sympathetic controls the body's level of arousal and the parasympathetic controls the body's level of relaxation. By extending the exhale the body is forced to relax more quickly.

Extension of the out breath

There are many breathing exercises which enable us to induce the state of relaxation but the optimum breathing rates are known as **7/11 breathing** which is where we breathe in to the count of seven and out to the count of eleven. Many people find it difficult at first to breathe in this manner unless they have been trained to do so, which is why 4/4 breathing is often easier in the first instance. However, it is a goal worth aspiring to, since it enables the body to downshift, causing it to operate in an economical way by conserving energy expenditure.

Correct breathing

Although breathing correctly is a process that we do quite instinctively as babies, sadly many of us lose this ability as we grow older. It is not uncommon to see shallow 'thoracic' breathing in the general adult population. By this I am referring to using the chest only for breathing, rather than deep abdominal breathing, which involves breathing into the belly. By pushing down the diaphragm we extend the abdominal cavity, enabling our lungs to fill up to full capacity.

It is easy to see if you are breathing correctly by initially lying on the floor with a book placed over your tummy. As you breathe in deeply the book should rise up and as you breathe out the book should slowly descend. By doing this, you will be ensuring that you are breathing correctly, as the book will scarcely move if you are breathing shallowly, only using your upper chest.

Start off by doing 4/4 breathing and then gradually build this up towards 7/11 breathing. Each person has their own natural speed of breathing, so do not be worried if you find 4/4 breathing to be too rapid for you and start further up the scale, for example breathing in to the count of five and out to the count of six.

---

3. Relax
Control muscle tension

> *I live for Pilates reformer class. I go at least three*
> *times a week. It's a great way to lengthen your*
> *muscles, stretch, and kind of relax your mind.*
> Shawn Johnson

A tense body equates to a tense mind
We all know that it is impossible to feel totally relaxed when our body feels tense and rigid. We need to address this tension in order to promote a sense of well-being and comfort. As you now know, the brain interprets tension in the body as a response to being in the presence of a physical threat.

Fighting stance
You only have to look at the stance of two combatants as they face off against each other to see how this works. Their bodies become rigid and angular, jaws jut out, fists are clenched and the upper body leans forward in a locked and aggressive manner. This is all part of the fight or flight

response, which enables us to adopt a threatening and menacing pose to dissuade any would-be attacker from coming too close.

As always, this is an excellent response if we truly are under physical threat, but when dealing with a phobia this is not the case. The interpretation of threat is irrational and therefore our tense musculature is causing our body to be flooded with more and more stress hormones. As you now know so well, if the hormones are not put to use in enabling you to flee or fight, it will only result in greater discomfort as the physical symptoms you experience are ramped up.

Muscle relaxation exercises

The answer is to remove the tension and allow our muscles to relax. We can do this by means of **targeted muscle relaxation exercises** or what are known as **progressive muscle relaxation exercises**. These exercises consist of tensing the muscle first then relaxing it so that the contrast of tension and relaxation can be keenly felt by the body. In addition, by tensing the muscles in this accentuated manner, the blood and toxins which have congregated in the tense muscle are mechanically pumped out, enabling the muscle to become smooth and comfortable.

Targeted muscle relaxation
This is a useful exercise if we readily know the areas in our body that are prone to holding

tension. Many people tend to hold tension in their neck muscles; many others have very tense back muscles. Once you have located your tense muscles, tighten them even further to the count of four and then to the count of four release this tension as much as you can, allowing the muscles to deeply relax. Do this several times until the area of tension feels comfortable and relaxed. Then re-scan your body to discover if there are any other areas that feel tense and repeat the process by targeting each area in turn as above.

Progressive muscle relaxation
This exercise takes longer but results in a fully relaxed body. In a similar way to the previous exercise, tense and relax each muscle group in turn to the count of four before moving on to the next group of muscles in your body. You can start at your head or feet and gradually work through all the muscle groups in a systematic and progressive manner until you reach the other end of your body. It is advisable to do this exercise while lying down or sitting up in a comfortable chair in which you feel fully supported.

It is an excellent idea to try to get into the habit of doing a progressive muscle relaxation exercise[1] on a regular basis, once or twice a week. This will not only help to improve your ability to sleep but will also make your body less prone to

---

[1] Detailed muscle exercises can be found in my book, *Flying with Confidence: The Proven Programme To Fix Your Flying Fears.*

panicking inappropriately. Deep muscle relaxation, as with slow rhythmical breathing, enables your body to downshift and recalibrate the fight or flight response so that it becomes less 'trigger happy' and less likely to fire off inappropriately.

4. Rehearse
Control your thoughts

> *Imagination is everything. It is the preview of life's coming attractions.*
> Albert Einstein

Constructive use of your imagination

Once you have regained a calm mind and relaxed body it is important that it remains that way. You can prevent yourself from repeating the panic cycle by harnessing your imagination to your advantage. You do this by actively choosing what you wish to think about. By choosing to reflect upon a relaxing, happy scene, your mind will continue to remain calm and relaxed.

Misuse of your imagination

This is the reverse of what you have done in the past when you have allowed your phobia gremlin to employ your imagination to conjure up all manner of distressing scenes – you simply need to train yourself to imagine a more positive, calming one.

The more vivid and detailed you make the relaxing scene the busier your brain will be in conjuring up this manifestation in your mind's eye. By focusing on each sense in turn you can build a vibrant image made up of smell, taste, touch, sight and sound which creates a huge distraction for the mind to focus upon. Whilst doing this there is little room left for your phobia gremlin to sow the seeds of panic and anxiety.

Locked trance state

By harnessing our imagination we are using what is known as the brain's trance state, which enables us to lock our attention away from the feared phobic stimulus. So if you are afraid of public speaking you can imagine that the people in the audience are just a group of your friends. Or if you are sitting on a crowded bus and suffer from claustrophobia you can imagine that you are sitting in your own comfy, spacious armchair at home.

Many sportspeople use the state of locked attention to visualize their finest match or best goal, to both calm them down and get them in touch with their abilities and resources before competing.

The state of locked attention has been experienced by many of us when we have been so absorbed in what we are doing that we have not noticed how cold or hungry we have become. It is not until something has roused us from this absorbed state that we become aware of pain or tiredness. It is this locked state of attention which enables people to receive painful medical treatment without the intervention of an anaesthetic.

Practise using your imagination

Below I have included a visualization exercise, to enable you to put your imagination into action. The best guided visualization you can use is to focus on a happy scene from your own past which you will be able to conjure up at will. This will enable you to relax and prevent frightening negative thoughts and images from intruding. The nature of this scene is entirely down to you and it does not need to be peaceful and tranquil. The memory must simply be pleasant and positive which will make you feel confident and contented.

 Imagine you are strolling through a fairground on a crisp winter's evening. Try to summon up in your mind's eye all the sights, sounds, sensations, smells and tastes that I am about to describe to you. Before you start, make sure that you are breathing correctly, to make this experience more powerful and relaxing.

Read each paragraph in turn then close your eyes and try to imagine the scene in your mind's eye before moving on to the next paragraph.

1. First, picture the lively, buzzing scene before you. There is a visual feast of bright garish lights illuminating the colourful rides, such as the waltzers, big wheel and carousel. Notice the mixture of striking primary colours,

soft candy shades and multi-coloured stripes of the banners and bunting fluttering from the numerous stalls.

2. Now bring your attention to the cacophony of different noises you are hearing as venders call out their wares and fairground folk entreat you to sample their rides. Above all of this, you can hear the high-pitched squeals of delight, coming from overhead, as the excited youngsters loop-the-loop on the big dipper.

3. Feel the harsh, rough hairiness of the coconut you have just won. Now, in total contrast, stroke the soft plush velvety fur of the cuddly toy you have been awarded for your accurate marksmanship on the firing range.

4. Next, try to summon up the tempting aroma of hot dogs and onions sizzling on the grill close by. Or perhaps you feel more drawn to the evocative smell of candy floss being spun into voluminous, brightly coloured whirls?

5. Finally, see if you can conjure up in your mind's eye the delicious sweetness as you bite into the hard outer casing of a toffee apple and then savour the sharp bitter juiciness of the fruit within. If this doesn't tempt your palate, then imagine the distinctive salty, warm buttery taste of freshly made popcorn.

With this technique, the important thing is to experiment, use your imagination, and find out what works for you.

Reflections

Ask yourself the following questions:

1. How did you get on with using your imagination?

2. Were you able to filter out other distractions and absorb yourself in the descriptions?

3. What real memories can you bring to mind of happy scenes from your own past?

4. Choose one of these memories and describe who else is in the scene with you, what you are doing, where it takes place and why it is so positive and pleasant.

To summarize the 4Rs Paradigm

The instant you recognize that you are feeling anxious and panicky, take immediate steps to:

React by telling yourself that you are not going down that route and say a positive affirmation to yourself.

Regulate by getting your breathing under control, ensuring that it is slow and measured.

Relax by ensuring all muscle groups are stretched and relaxed to relieve any tension.

Rehearse by using your imagination to invoke a positive happy scene upon which you can dwell until the anxiety has passed.

The 4Rs Paradigm will enable you to remain calm whilst confronting your phobia. For many people, the knowledge that they can now control their anxiety will be sufficient in itself to dissolve their phobia; this is because it is more the fear of the panic attack than the phobia per se that has alarmed them. For others, recovery may be incremental and take longer before a phobia-free existence is established.

Balanced lifestyle to stay phobia free

Regardless of the category into which you fall, it is important that once you have conquered your phobia you live your life in such a way that you will be able to remain phobia free. What I mean by this is that you adopt a balanced lifestyle, which will include: exercising, eating a healthy diet and investing in regular relaxation on a daily basis. This will not only reduce your likelihood of becoming a target for a phobia or other mental health problems but will also enhance your physical health and well-being enormously.

Balance is another word for harmony, which consists of stretching sufficiently so that you feel challenged and engaged with life, while also recognising that the mind and the body need play and relaxation to generate the fuel which drives your creativity.

17. Final Word

Life without liberty is like a body without spirit.
Khalil Gibran

In concluding this book I would like to remind you of my opening words, which were that *each of us possesses huge reservoirs of untapped resources.* If you are suffering from a phobia I invite you to address it as soon as possible by tapping into those resources. Sadly, many people in the world do not have the freedom to live their life in accordance with their choices and beliefs.

We largely enjoy the liberty to live our lives unencumbered by the decrees of dictators and despots. I personally feel that it is our duty to live our lives to the full; quite simply because we can. What a tragedy that despite enjoying these opportunities of freedom and liberty we allow ourselves to become chained and incarcerated by psychological dictators and despots such as phobia gremlins.

I urge you to recognize your personal power and refuse to dance to your phobia's tune any longer. Face the fear, and take your life back.

'I' have the power
An *aide memoire* for confronting your phobia

Initiate a resourceful approach to challenging your fear

Identify your phobia triggers

Interrogate the evidence justifying your fear

Intercept your frightening thoughts

Implement a slow, measured breathing pattern

Induce a state of muscle relaxation

Imagine a positive scenario

Interpret your fear realistically

Inculcate a new constructive response to phobia triggers

I have conquered my phobia and am free to live my life.

Rightful liberty is unobstructed action according to our will.
Thomas Jefferson

I hope that you have found the contents of this little book of use in helping you or someone else to overcome a phobia. I wish all my readers health, happiness and humour in their phobia-free future.

Useful Contacts

UK

Alcoholics Anonymous
Tel: 08457 697 555
www.alcoholics-anonymous.org.uk

Anxiety UK
Tel: 08444 775 774
Email: info@anxietyuk.org.uk

British Airways Flying with Confidence
http://flyingwithconfidence.com

British Association for Behavioural and Cognitive Therapies
Tel: 0161 705 4304
Email: babcp@babcp.com

British Association for Counselling and Psychotherapy
Tel: 01455 883316
Email: bacp@bacp.co.uk

British Psychological Society
Tel: 0116 254 9568
Email: enquiry@bps.org.uk

Guided Relaxation Resources
Tel: 07957 797490
www.widenmind.com

Human Givens
www.humangivens.com

International Stress Management Association
Tel: 0845 680 7083
Email: stress@isma.org.uk

The Mental Health Foundation
Tel: 020 7803 1100
Email: mhf@mhf.org.uk

Mind
Tel: 0300 123 3393
Email: info@mind.org.uk

National Counselling Society
Tel: 0870 850 3389
www.NationalCounsellingSociety.org

No Panic
Tel: 0808 808 0545
Email: ceo@nopanic.org.uk

Patricia Furness-Smith
01494 766246
www.maturus.co.uk

The Sleep Council
Tel: 0800 018 7923
Email: info@sleepcouncil.com

UK Psychological Trauma Society
Email: UKPTSinfo@googlemail.com

Canada
Canadian Mental Health Association
http://www.cmha.ca/

The Canadian Association of Cognitive and Behavioural Therapies
http://cacbt.ca/en/index.htm

Canadian Psychological Association/ Sociétié Canadienne de Psychologie
+1-613-237-2144
http://www.cpa.ca/

Anxiety Disorders Association of Canada
contactus@anxietycanada.ca
1-888-223-2252
http://www.anxietycanada.ca/english/index.php

South Africa
The South African Depression and Anxiety Group
011 262 6396
http://www.sadag.org/

Selfgrow Development Group
+27 021 555-4248
http://www.selfgrow.co.za/

Psychological Society of South Africa
+27-486-3322
http://www.psyssa.com/

South African National Association of Practicing Psychologists
+27-11-485-2596
http://sanapp.co.za/

Australia
Australian Association for Cognitive and Behaviour Therapy
http://www.aacbt.org/

The Australian Psychological Society Ltd
+61-3-8662-3300
http://www.psychology.org.au/

New Zealand
New Zealand Psychological Society
+64-4-473-4884
http://www.psychology.org.nz/cms_display.php

USA
American Psychological Association
+1-202-336-6024
http://www.apa.org/

Association for Psychological Science
+1-202-293-9300
http://www.psychologicalscience.org/

US National Committee for Psychology
+1-202-334-2807
http://sites.nationalacademies.org/PGA/biso/index.htm

Scotland
Counselling & Psychotherapy in Scotland
01786 475 140
http://www.cosca.org.uk/

Ireland
Psychological Society of Ireland
+353-1-472-0105
http://www.psihq.ie/

Acknowledgements

I would like to first and foremost thank all of my courageous clients and students who have been willing to share with me their struggles with phobias. I am grateful for their openness and candour and the deep trust which they have invested in me. I am particularly indebted to those who took the trouble to send me a synopsis of their experiences in dealing with their respective phobias. Sadly, in order to preserve their privacy and anonymity, I cannot mention them by name, but they know who they are and they have my deep gratitude.

I would also like to thank clinical psychologists Dr Mark Laskin and Dr Charlotte Wing, along with general practitioners Dr Una Carleen and Dr Laura Lewis for their much-welcomed input. My sincere gratitude goes to Gwen Milligan for her excellent secretarial support. I would also like to thank my editor Kate Hewson and assistant editor Nira Begum for their expertise and encouragement in putting this book together. My gratitude also goes to Mark Ecob for his design for the book cover. I am of course enormously grateful to Icon Books for giving me this opportunity to demystify the world of phobias.

As always, I am eternally grateful for my parents' continued enthusiasm and interest in all of my projects. I am also indebted to Cringer, Bonje and Rapseybell for all the wisdom I have gleaned in their delightful company. Finally, I would like to acknowledge Aleeze, Sweet and Rudge for all the love, laughter and light which they bring into my life; there are no grey days in their presence.

Appendix

Hierarchy of fears in claustrophobia

Spend fifteen minutes in a room without windows with the door ajar	1
Visit an empty cinema and sit in the middle of a row	1
Stand on a train platform at off-peak time	1
Step inside a large empty lift and then come straight out	2
Sit in the back seat of a stationary car	2
Spend fifteen minutes in a windowless room with the door closed	3
Take a short journey as a passenger sitting in the back of a car	4
Get into a large empty lift and go up to the first floor	4
Take a ride on a bus for one stop and sit by the door	5
Spend 30 minutes in a small windowless room with the door closed	5
Go into a small empty lift and go to the first floor	6
Stand on train platform when it is busy	6
Take a short ride on a train when it is not busy	6
Go into a large lift with other people and go to the first floor	7

Go to the cinema when it is not busy and sit on the outside seat	7
Get into a large empty lift and go to the top floor	8
Take a 30-minute drive as a passenger in the back sear of a car	8
Do one junction on the motorway as a passenger in the front	9
Go in a small lift to the top floor with other people present	10
Do several junctions on the motorway	10
Take a train ride when it is busy	10
Take a bus ride when it is busy	10
Visit a crowded cinema and sit in the middle of a row	10

Index